The Presentation Survival Skills Guide

When time is short, the message is critical, and your creative juices are running on empty

Jim Endicott
Scott W. Lee, Ph.D.

Distinction Publishing

The Presentation Survival Skills Guide

Copyright © 2001 by Jim Endicott, Scott W. Lee

Distinction Publishing
18340 NE Rainbow Lane
Newberg, OR 97132

ISBN 0-9706727-0-5

All rights reserved. No part of this publication may be reproduced, stored in a retrieval system, or transmitted in any form or by any means – electronic, mechanical, photocopy, recording, or any other – except for brief quotations in printed reviews, without the prior permission of the authors and publisher.

Book layout by Dan Underhill
Cover design by Jim Endicott
Cartoon illustrations by Paul Lanquist

Printed in the United States of America

For Jeremy James Endicott, my son, whose memory, personal courage and fierce faith in God continues to challenge and cheer me on from his home in heaven.
- Jim

Special thanks to…
From Jim…
Diana & Amy Endicott for their unconditional love, prayers and encouragement for a very busy husband and father. Debbi Anderson for her efforts in the editing process. Dan Underhill for his assistance in layout and design mixed with positive words of support and encouragement and to Karyn Crawford for her patience, confidence and prayers.

From Scott…
Joan, Marissa and Brooks Lee for their patience and playfulness to keep me encouraged during this work. And most significantly, I would like to thank Jim for extending his friendship beyond our fishing trips to rendezvous in the adventurous thoughts and creativity of this book.

Table of Contents

Introduction .... *v*

Survival Skill #1
Create the Game Plan 1
- *The five-minute presentation pre-plan* 2
- *Who's going to show up to deliver the presentation?* 7

Survival Skill #2
Prepare for Your Audience 13
- *Four things your audiences demand of you* 14
- *The most critical five minutes* 17
- *Prepare a strong closing message* 21

Survival Skill #3
Shape the Message 25
- *Say it with pictures* 26
  Right-brain content in a left-brain world.
- *Premier storytelling* 29
  How every good presentation is a well-told story.
- *Personal stories* 34
  Your most powerful presentation tool.

Survival Skill #4
Craft the Images 37
- *Templates* 39
- *Base artwork* 41
- *Animation* 45
- *Fonts* 46
- *Color* 48

Table of Contents

Sound and video 49
Managing a collaborative presentation effort ..54

Survival Skill #5
Gain the Mental Presentation Edge 61

Envisioning success 62

Dealing with fear 65
Managing the beast within.

When you go blank 68
Quick recovery technique.

The "2-minute drill" for presenters 72
When your presentation is cut short.

Survival Skill #6
Manage Your Presentation Environment .79

Use environment-compatible graphics 80

Line of sight – point of focus 82

Manage your presentation technology 85

Manage room sound 88

Manage room lighting 89

Environmental overload 90

Survival Skill #7
Hone the Art of Presenting 95

The important role of coaches/mentors 96

Get up to bat as often as you can! 99

Set your graphics standards high 100
Get your creativity out-of-the-box.

Learn from the presentation design pros 102

Exceeding your "personal best" efforts 105

Survival Skill #8
Create and Deliver Internet-based Presentations 109
- *Options for web-based presentations* 110
- *Designing good Internet presentation templates* .113
- *Unique content development requirements* ..115
- *Delivering Internet presentations* 117

Survival Skill #9
Survive Q&A Sessions 123
- *The "co-presenter"* 125
- *Stump the presenter* 126
- *Men are from Mars, women, boys, cats, dogs* ..127
- *"Excuse me, I wasn't listening"* 128

Survival Skill #10
Understand Your Ultimate Strength 131

Appendix 137
Survival guide to presentation terminology.

Introduction

Introduction

Everyday in America, people from every walk of life find themselves in front of an audience presenting their thoughts and ideas. Sometimes the stakes are huge. Other times the opportunities may not be profound or life changing, but they are always intensely personal. For business professionals, educators and others, the process related to creating and delivering a compelling presentation is often fraught with frustration. Never has the need for such an essential life skill permeated the world of business and personal life so completely.

The Survival Guide offers up some practical insight into the secrets of creating great presentations – start to finish! You'll quickly find in these pages the critical fundamentals needed to approach the process of message development, graphics and design. Although most books end there, the Survival Guide goes on to tap into the experiences of a psychologist to shed some light on the frequently misunderstood areas of how and why audiences learn, retain information and take action. His answers just might surprise you.

There's one other thing we can say for certain, most presenters lack the one essential ingredient critical to their personal development…time. There's never enough time to pick up more relevant skills, time to think through the process of creating a better message, or essential time to seriously hone the art of presenting. We can't create more time, but we can find tools that help us pick up essential skills when we need them.

All the elements you need to elevate the impact of your next presentation are now available in one easy-to-read reference book. If the introduction strikes a bit close to home, then the Survival Guide was created just for you. Its quick reference format puts essential presentation concepts at your fingertips to help you not only survive your next big presentation, but truly excel.

The Survival Guide features:

A Closer Look
More detailed tips and ideas for your next presentation.

Case Studies
See how other presenters handled their presentation challenges.

Shrink Wrap
A psychologist's perspective on impact, audiences and you.

Survival Summaries
A quick overview of critical presentation tips.

The Survival Skills Guide may not make you an overnight success but it will provide you with practical tips and insights to make your next presentation just that much easier. So stick this in your briefcase; it just may become one of your most influential traveling companions.

"The best leaders... almost without exception and at every level, are master users of stories and symbols."

– Tom Peters

Survival Skill 1

Create the Presentation Game Plan

Hardly anything gets accomplished without a solid plan. Sports teams study their opponents and come up with a sound strategy. Businessmen and women plan for acquisitions, partnerships and account strategies. They all go through a planning process because the lack of a plan often spells disaster or at best mediocrity. Despite all this planning, however, one area has sadly lacked much pre-planning, even though the stakes for failure are enormous… our presentations. Survival Skill #1 will explain how to put together the pieces that create a successful presentation. It starts with an understanding of your audience and ends with a decision about how you will personally approach the presentation process.

The five-minute presentation pre-plan

A quick process for planning the presentation message, graphics and flow.

Who's going to show up to deliver the presentation?

Just be yourself because perfect presenters are rarely the best presenters.

Skill #1 – Create the Presentation Game Plan

"Getting ready is the secret to success."
– Henry Ford

A Closer Look...

Here's the detail you need to truly fine-tune your presentation development process using a presentation planning document.

- Initiate each new presentation project with a presentation pre-plan so the presenter, co-presenters and designers are on the "same page" from the start.

- As an internal design tool, teams can identify platform or context-related design issues early on. (ie. Is the presentation going to be used for both laptop and web presentations?)

- Event planning is enhanced by knowing that a presentation requires house sound or video support. Think ahead and make the right contacts.

- Eliminate the "we didn't know" phenomenon by using the planner as a basis for creating your own design/event specification document.

The Presentation Planner
Background dynamics:

Date/time: _____

Title or theme: _____

Subtitle: _____

Length of presentation in minutes: _____

What are the stakes? This will affect all other decisions! _____

Primary presentation medium: _____
(Slides, overheads, electronic, other)

Do you have a back-up medium planned?
No / Yes: _____

Handouts required?
(HANDOUT more than you say, SAY more than you PROJECT)

No / Yes: _____

Audience profiling
Describe your audience:

(Engineers, executives, high tech, low tech, conservative…)

_____
_____

What are their expectations? How can you exceed these expectations?

_____
_____

Anticipated questions or challenges:

_____
_____

If you delivered the "perfect" presentation, what would your target audience do with the information you just delivered?

_____
_____

4 | Skill #1 – Create the Presentation Game Plan

Bottom-line message

If they will only remember three or four things from your presentation, what would you want those messages to be?

1) _____
2) _____
3) _____
4) _____

Can't seem to narrow it down to less than eight or ten? Guess what? Your audience most likely won't remember any of them!

Create your closing summary slide(s) first!

Content benchmarks

I. Personal introduction highlights

Keep it brief and make who you are relevant to what they want.

_____

_____

A good title slide communicates essential context. Avoid the obvious, like "Presented to" and the date.

II. Agenda milestones

Simple, concise, cohesive. Create clear roadmaps.

_____

_____

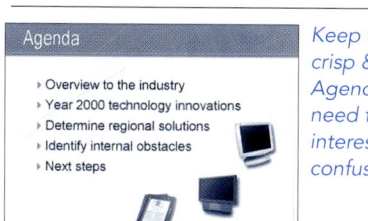

Keep the agenda crisp & clear. Agenda slides need to create interest, not confusion.

III. Develop strong opening comments

Bridges are built right here and now. Your opening remarks will either build immediate relational/topical connections with your audience or create obstacles for the rest of your presentation. Get your audience thinking. Engage their minds and hearts.

Personal story _____

Relevant quote_____

Information impact on audience _____

Unanticipated outcomes _____

IV. High-level message development

Creating a clear outline that concludes with your three or four closing points is the fulfillment of a silent commitment to your audience. First, lay out your presentation TITLES only. Does the flow of your titles create a crisp and logical path through the content? To this end, change the order. Delete noncritical segments. Drive to your conclusion at every opportunity. Once your titles are just right, drill down to the next level of detail. Create the basic text messages that support the title. As a final step, augment the text with appropriate graphical support (charts, pictures, screen captures, illustrations, etc.).

Case Study

A large national contingent services client of mine was in trouble. They were losing multimillion dollar staffing contracts and their presentations were only a part of the problem. An independent consulting exercise discovered what was really going on. When 12 members of their top regional and national sales teams were interviewed, they were asked, "What three or four top key messages do you want every prospect to understand about you?" The results yielded no less then 22 different core messages that ranged from the very general to the overly specific. **There was no consensus, so the company's "story" was constantly being told differently.** Blind interviews with those on the receiving end of their presentations yielded the same ambiguity regarding the staffing company's real identity and strengths.

A day-long planning session with senior managers started with each putting four sticky notes on a board and explaining why their key message ideas were valid. True to expectation, 18-20 different messages filled the board. Then they were asked to see if reoccurring themes restated in different ways were present. The notes were then reorganized into five basic themes. Some key messages turned out to be simply the "ante to play" statements in their industry and were not differentiating statements. (For example, National Presence.) Those were set aside. Next, a brainstorming session shaped the actual description of each grouping. Four key messages were now produced and the individual notes became a majority of the slide content that supported each theme. Mission accomplished!

Shrink Wrap
Dr. Scott Lee
Who's going to show up to deliver the presentation?

Be yourself because perfect presenters are rarely the best presenters.

Slick Willie, a used car salesmen, and an overdressed date all have in common one dominant theme: they're not believable. Their agenda is not in the audience's best interest. Anything too good, too pretty or too smooth "is too good to be true." Audiences believe the same thing about presenters. Our well-honed defenses screen out material we have learned to not be trustworthy. The following case illustrates this reality.

Case Study
Mismatched Socks

In the late 1960's, the United State's involvement in the Viet Nam War was highly controversial. A university study used this issue as a means of measuring presentation effectiveness. A debate was arranged between two well-rehearsed student speakers, one pro and one con. The arguments were memorized, the participants were dressed similarly in identical size outfits, and the debate was then presented six times to freshman classes. During the day, arguments were reversed, clothes were swapped, and positions were rotated to control for individual differences. Most significantly, during each presentation, one of the participants wore mismatched socks (navy blue and black). Even the socks were rotated so that each debater had his chance with the mismatched socks.

At the end of the day, the results of the debates revealed significant agreement of each audience. The presenter that wore the mismatched socks was overwhelmingly favored by the audience. It's likely the audience felt a stronger connection to that presenter. He was considered easier to relate to and more believable because of his flaws, not despite them.

All things being equal, we connect with, understand better, and believe more someone who has small flaws—like we do. But be careful; only when there is genuine audience respect for the presenter does the issue of a revealed weakness add believability.

Key Audience Connection Tips

- **Identify with the audience**

    Relate to the audience, don't put yourself above them. You don't need a perfect message. You need a strong, relevant and personal message to come alongside an audience.

- **Build respect**

    Work hard in your preparation to be real and relevant.

- **Imperfections**

    When something goes wrong, don't make excuses for imperfections.

- **Mistakes**

    If you make a mistake, correct it and go on.

- **Make it personal**

    Bring personal stories, messages, and humor to your presentation.

    Maybe the lesson here isn't to go directly to your sock drawer (ladies, you have a unique challenge here) and put on the most ridiculous pair of socks you can find. There's a difference between being approachable and being stupid, but the principle is sound. Audiences aren't looking for perfection, just a warm and approachable you.

Survival Summaries
- **Understand the backdrop behind the presentation**

    Get your arms around the issues and actions that surround your presentation.

    - **What are the stakes for your presentation?** Your answer will dictate the tools used, resources allocated, as well as the time to craft the message.

    - **What is the context?** What's the theme of the presentation? How are other presenters addressing their related content?

    - **How much time do you have?** Create content to fill 90% of the time allotted. Rushing the closing

Skill #1 – Create the Presentation Game Plan

minutes of your presentation only means key points and critical summary statements get lost.

- **Audience profiling**

   Have a clear understanding of the filters that will sift your presentation message.

   - **Know the audience you're stuffing.** Talk to audience members ahead of time; understand their expectations, perspectives, fears and passions.
   - **Presentation detail is a function of audience expectations.** A room full of senior managers will mostly likely be looking for summary detail while a tradeshow seminar might require more details, illustrations and validation.

- **Bottom-line message**

   When presentations are created without regard to a core message, they meander, confuse and overwhelm audiences.

   - **Distill your presentation down to 3-4 key messages.** Presentation length is a by-product of how extensive the supporting detail is under each of your key presentation messages. Content that doesn't support those messages should be scrutinized for appropriateness.

- **Content benchmarks**

   Just as every well-told story has common elements, so does a well-crafted presentation. Sensory-based content, with a mix of elements, makes for great presentations. Don't forget a strong opening and convincing closing elements.

Key presentation elements:

Title slide — Establish credibility, relevance, and context

Opener — Opening statement or story that imparts topic relevance

Agenda — Provide clear direction for the audience

Base content — Balance text with relevant and appropriate supporting graphics

Close — Summary statement or story that restates key messages in a way that fosters retention and deeper audience connections

Survival Skill 2

Prepare for Your Audience

If all you did was just sit around and deliver your presentations in a mirror, you might find yourself pretty enamored with yourself. Real audiences, however, are not as easy to impress. They expect some pretty clear things from you and you'd better deliver! It's not that they want you to fail. To the contrary, they want you to succeed. They simply expect that you've put more effort into the presentation than they spent in just getting there.

Four things your audiences demand of you
Put yourself in your audience's shoes and ask these questions of yourself.

The most critical five minutes
A strong presentation opening and closing are critical to locking in an audience and being remembered for all the right reasons.

Prepare a strong closing message
A strong conclusion is often remembered long after you leave.

Skill #2 – Prepare For Your Audience

> "Great public speakers listen to the audience with their eyes. They exhaust neither the topic nor the audience" – H.H. Brackenridge

A Closer Look...
Your audience will demand four things from you:

➡ *Do you really know your stuff?*

There's no substitute for a knowledgeable presenter. The old axiom, "fake it until you make it" just doesn't cut it when it comes to your presentations. Audiences are way too smart for presenters who try to bluff their way through a topic. Do your homework. Look for unique angles. Dig deeper into the subject to uncover supporting information, quotes, statistics and perspectives. Find third-party sources that validate your point of view.

➡ *Do you have any idea who you're stuffing?*

It's pretty tough creating relevant content if you're clueless as to what your audience is looking for. Perhaps you're fortunate to know your audience thoroughly; but for most presenters, a little homework is in order. Here are three quick ways to qualify who will actually be sitting out there staring back at you.

▸ **Interview several individuals who will be attending...**

- "Why are you coming?"
- "What would you consider a 'successful' event?"
- "What would exceed your expectations?"
- "What three things would you want to understand better when you leave?"

- **Cruise the Internet to research their company, association or business interest.** Demonstrate that knowledge during the presentation with company or industry statistics, knowledge of key players, or some recent news about the industry. It only takes a few references to create a perception of specific industry/association knowledge.

- **Talk to someone who has presented to that group before.** Ask what worked well and what didn't, and what they would do differently?

➡ *Be sensitive to when they're really stuffed.*

Frequently, presenters try to jam too much content into too little time. Let me suggest something a bit radical. Create content that only fills 90% of the time. You heard me. For good presentation content to be "digestible" by an audience they need processing time. If your pace is rapid or if the content is heavy, you will lose your opportunity to be memorable. Good handouts are helpful in archiving reference information but if you don't provide breathing room to assimilate visual content, you run the risk the audience won't find it later. We're not talking long dramatic pauses but rather a reasonable amount of well-paced content that leaves your audience wanting just a bit more.

➡ *They really don't want to see the same old stuff.*

There's no such thing as status-quo presentations. Either you stand out on the merits of a clean and graphically well-illustrated business story, or you blend into a sea of mediocrity by looking like most other presenters. What makes the difference?

Skill #2 – Prepare For Your Audience

- **Unique look.** Create a professional and unique template framework for your presentation. Integrate elements that are industry or topic relevant. Avoid stock template looks like the plague.

- **Unique approach.** Don't take the easy way out of presentation development by using screen after screen of bulleted text. Convert text to graphical or sensory-based content at every opportunity. 80% of all general audiences process graphical information much easier. 85+% of all presentations you'll see are predominately text. Integrate images, clean and simple charts, and relevant photos to build concepts on screen. Want to know what's professional? Take a look at a good brochure. You won't find clipart, misaligned or flat colored boxes, or oversized graphics.

- **Unique theme-oriented presentations.** Specific presentation themes can help set an engaging context for a presentation. Make sure you can tie it in, but look for interesting ways to leverage the theme. In a recent presentation in Chicago to an agency of the Park and Recreation departments, the conference planners tied into an article that I'd written entitled, "When fishing or presenting, it pays to use the right bait." This article (distributed as a conference handout) became a focal point for the event. I was able to open with a (real) fishing story with clear topic connectivity as well as supplemental seminar themes that leveraged the topic metaphor while relating it back to presenting.

    Know why the fish won't bite. Know your audience inside and out"

    "**Using the right bait.** Selecting good presentation graphics"

"**Knowing where to fish**: Targeting appropriate content to your audience."

The storyline was the glue that held the themes together.

♦ **Unique delivery.** Voice quality, pacing, body language and audience interaction come with practice and experience. Be a bit unpredictable. Your audience can't arrive at the end of your presentation before you do. If you're serious about honing the art of presenting, you'll seek out peer coaches that will tell you the truth about how you're perceived during a presentation.

Case Study

In Hawaii, presenter John Pierce, an executive with a major workers' compensation insurance underwriter, was delivering a presentation focused on communicating workplace safety to a group of clients. His focus: the tools related to on-the-job safety. To make things a bit more interesting, John sported a leather tool belt and a plaid shirt and leveraged a presentation template reminiscent of the television show Home Improvement. John's presentation was voted the most memorable and educational of the weekend. Could we do any better than that?

The most critical five minutes of any presentation

Whether you like it or not, audiences form opinions early on in your presentations. In the critical first two to three minutes, your opening comments, story or introduction will either engage and build anticipation into an audience or send them the clear message your presentation is the same old stuff they've seen before. You've got two

Skill #2 – Prepare For Your Audience

minutes to answer these questions <u>from your audience's perspective:</u>

- "Is this information important and relevant to me?"
- "Will it be told in a way that will be interesting?"
- "How much creativity and effort has gone into this presentation?"
- "Do I have a good feeling about this person presenting?"

The closing two to three minutes are the equivalent of a gymnast's high bar dismount. This is no more apparent than when the world watches the Olympic gymnast carefully execute this demanding moment. You can sense the anxiety of the crowd as the set of required moves are completed and the gymnast accelerates for the critical dismount. Even the best routine can be unraveled if the dismount is sloppy or the gymnast wavers in the execution. Simply just slowing down and hanging lifelessly from the high bar and dropping to the ground would be inexcusable. As anticlimactic as that would be, presenters everyday commit the presentation equivalent of the slow down and drop maneuver. The presentation nears the end and concludes abruptly because time is over. The summary and relational hooks that tie all the presentation pieces together are omitted. The critical "dismount" never occurs. Presenters must treat the conclusion as the last final impression; story, statement, quote and conclusions as well-orchestrated final elements. We'll deal more with how you can create a strong closing later in this section.

TIP: To control the audience's focal point, consider hitting the B key on your laptop keyboard while in PowerPoint/Show to temporarily black out the screen. Now 100% of the focus is directed to you during those important opening and closing statements. Hitting the B key again restores your presentation on screen.

Shrink Wrap
Dr. Scott Lee
The Power of Strong Starts & Finishes

In psychology, we refer to the significance of the beginning and the ending as the law of **primacy** and **recency**. The brain recognizes new material as interesting and it stands out from the background "noise" that the brain has become accustomed to. Therefore, the beginning of a presentation has a great opportunity to be encoded as pertinent material due to its sense of newness. **The brain wakes** up during this part of the message and this alertness allows us to remember more.

To the brain, the middle of the presentation feels a lot like similar material, "same old same old," or background noise to be filtered out. The brain pleasantly drifts away…making the middle material difficult to remember.

The finish is the last impression to the brain as it naturally wakes up again with a transition to a break, the next speaker, etc. When we mention the words "finally" or "in conclusion," the audience wakes up, anticipating the change (not just because they are finished napping). Therefore the **ending sticks out in our memory**. Avoid those finishing words until you're clearly ready to transition. Attention will once again wane if you falter in the close.

Case Study
A note from Scott...

Many years ago when I was in high school swing choir, we would participate with other fine jazz groups in competitions. We would always hope to start or finish a competition because the winners regularly seemed to come from the beginning or the end. In a Reno competition, our position of singing last helped us stand out in the memory of the judges. They awarded the equivalent of two first place trophies: the first competitors and the last competitors.

Structuring your practice time

To create memorable presentations, invest your presentation practice time in these key areas:

30% Opening and closing remarks
Like a good movie, long after the actions over, audiences will remember those first and last impressions as they recall events.

20% Technology
As much as we may like our laptop computers and electronic projectors, they are not what our presentations are all about. The less comfortable we are with technology, however, the more we inadvertently put those elements between us and our audience. For example, presenters who point their remote pointing devices at the laptop like a phaser can create unnecessary fanfare around the enabling technology. With a little practice, the remote pointing device can simply become an extension of your arm and can trigger the advance of presentation slides without the audience's awareness.

50% Smooth slide transitions supported by seamless verbal commentary.

Avoid abrupt starts and stops between slides. Seek to provide the audience with a seamless flowing commentary broken by logical topic transitions.

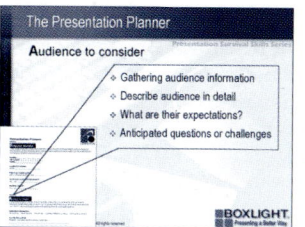

Build content on screen & "explode out" detail with a confident smooth flow

Prepare a strong closing message
How to conclude a dynamic presentation.

Gymnasts call it "sticking the landing," the final clean movement from the bar to the mat marking the successful conclusion of the routine.

Presenters often forget about this critical stage of their presentations. All the effort has gone into practicing the delivery of the individual screens; but when it comes to the final "pull it all together" conclusion of the presentation, many presenters seem to hang lifelessly from the bar. Here are some tips for sticking your presentation landing every time.

➡ **Tip #1 Create a crisp concise summary** of the presentation content so it's clear to everyone how it all fits together under a common theme or set of messages. If you can't do it in four or five bullets, perhaps your presentation is too "broad brush" and lacks actionable and discernable key points.

➡ **Tip #2 Step out of your presentation** by taking a few steps towards your audience; anchor yourself and deliver a personalization of the message through story that draws a clean parallel to the point of the presentation. Make it concise and don't ramble. Step back at your conclusion to signal the completion.

➡ **Tip#3 Leave them with a simple visual image** on screen that reinforces the words or images you've used to describe your content. One powerful relevant image is more memorable then a sea of bulleted summary statements left on screen. Summarize and reinforce with a strong visual image.

➡ **Tip#4 After your final words, pause and maintain eye contact** with your audience. Don't drop your eyes until you've acknowledged their applause. Thank them for their attention and participation. Be gracious and let them know how you will address questions and answers if appropriate.

Survival Summaries

Your opening and closing remarks will either engage your audience and build interest based on relevance and personal value, or cause them to strategize an early departure. Plan that critical time wisely.

• Do you really **know your stuff?**

You don't need to know everything. You do need to know what's important to your audience.

• Do you have any idea **who you're stuffing?**

Some web research and phone calls to prospective audience members can provide valuable insight into their needs. Demonstrate that knowledge of them during the presentation.

- Will you know **when they're stuffed?**

    Be aware of the time because you can bet they are. Create content to fill 90% of the allocated time to avoid a rushed introduction and summary.

- Are you prepared to show them **more than the same old stuff?**

    Audiences desperately want to experience fresh approaches to presentation graphics. Invest extra effort in graphics and more thoughtful content.

Spend 30% of your preparation time on the first and last five minutes of your presentation.

Audiences remember the beginning and ending elements of a presentation. Heavily invest your practice time in creating crisp and articulate introductions and concluding statements and stories.

Survival Skill 3

Shape the Message

We tend to want to put the presentation process in a class all by itself. After all, it leverages software used just for delivering presentations and it requires some skills we seldom use elsewhere. Presentation coaches offer insight on where to stand and how to gesture. Presentation design specialists provide guidance on the use of the graphics. It is a unique and new business communication art…or is it?

Communicating a compelling message to audiences is hardly new. There's much we can learn from those who've gone centuries before. You see, any really good presentation is just a well-told story. All the elements that enthrall grade school children in a public library on a Saturday morning are the same elements that engage a board of directors, a new strategic partner or a venture capitalist. Learn how your presentation stories are best illustrated and what every good "storyteller" would like you to know about presenting.

Say it with pictures
The challenge of creating left-brain content for a right-brain world.

Premier storytelling: The essence of every good presentation
How your presentations are just well-told stories.

Personal stories: Your most powerful presentation tool
Bridging experience with topic creates powerful connections.

"Creative minds have always been known to survive any kind of bad training."
— Anna Freud

Shrink Wrap
Dr. Scott Lee

Say it with pictures

I was standing in line at a Subway fast food restaurant when I observed to the person in front of me that the store ceiling fans were revolving in different directions. She replied that some were pulling up the cool air and others were pushing down the warm air. When I asked her how she remembered her thermodynamics so well, she stated, "High School Physics." When I commented that she had quite a memory, she told me something that struck me as a major key to audiences and presenters today. She said, "I remembered the experiments and the stories; I slept through the rest!"

This is true for many of us. We forget so much information and text-based knowledge; yet many years later we remember the stories and the experiments. I believe that this process is a function of the brain's method of learning.

The left hemisphere of the brain is responsible for figuring things out logically—it is the computer engineer within. Analysis of sequences, logical reasoning, verbal and writing skills, arithmetic, these functions are the domain of the left side. If you've ever crammed for a test, you probably used your left brain to process that information. The problem is, it takes a lot of studying—usually all night—to learn a little bit. We're bored because we have no meaningful, gut-level connection to the material, and then we forget most of the information as soon as we take the test. Not a very effective drive down that information highway.

- **Text-based presentations,** those that predominantly use words and written material to communicate, create a similar response in us. The left brain, which tends to be a bit suspicious of new learning, puts the information through several analytic screens (defenses) and heavily filters the material. Little gets through, we get bored easily and the material presented moves into short term memory at best.

- **Pictures & images** are processed quite differently in the right hemisphere. Here the brain uses sensory abilities to view the pictures (which we call graphical or imagistic input) and relates at a "gut level" or what we in psychology call "primary process" (unfiltered). In addition to its sensory awareness, the right side relates with our feelings and common experiences and therefore connects readily with the heart of the audience. Memory storage is longer-term because this picture material uses our own experience as a common reference point.

Let me illustrate using my daughter, Marissa. Imagine my desk having a picture frame around text material that says:

> - *Marissa*
> - *Age five*
> - *Girl*
> - *Blonde*
> - *Intelligent*
> - *Adventurous*

Those words are descriptive of my daughter, but a picture of her stomping in a mud puddle does so much more for me. Something inside me is touched when I see that picture because it relates to my personal experience. Pictures, stories and images build relational bridges that move our audiences to understanding and new behavior. I believe this is why we are presenting in the first place.

Marissa, having a wild, wet and wonderful adventure, connects with our own experiences.

A Closer Look...
Premier storytelling:
The essence of every good presentation
How your presentations are just well told stories

When our kids were growing up we learned many things about life. Sometimes we think that wisdom flows only one way during that time of life; however, to the astute parent, the lessons come unexpectedly and sometimes last a lifetime. For those of you who have had small children at home, you understand their attention span is not that different than the adults in a senior staff meeting or a prospective customer who only has 30 minutes to give you. The art of storytelling and keeping an audience engaged (no matter what their ages) is a life skill. Many of todays business presenters could learn a few things from good storytellers. Let's look at those elements that can make the difference between an average presentation and an exceptional one. It all starts at the very beginning...

Skill #3 – Shape the Message

The Opening:
"Once upon a time there was a dragon who tormented the villagers in a land far, far away."

Maybe you've heard the statistic that you have eight seconds to initially capture your audience's attention or you lose them forever. There's much truth to the urgent nature of setting a level of anticipation to what you have to say. All too often presentations begin abruptly with no attempt to create interest, buy in, or a sense of expectation. You just jump right in and hope that your title slide has said all there is to say. It doesn't work with kids and, I'm sorry to say, it rarely works with adults. Next time you begin your presentation, start with posing a question or making a statement that gets the audience's interest. "In a time of dramatically increasing business costs, I will provide you with three compelling ways you can consistently reduce your operating costs by 20% over the next 6 months." There's no substitute for a good introduction. As with children, however, you better deliver the goods.

The Passion:
"...and they ran as fast as their legs could take them; but the dragon got closer with every stride, the flare of his nostrils touched the back of their necks!"

A story told with little or no passion will leave an audience flat. I remember sitting through a budgeting meeting where two department managers were proposing expenditures for the next year. They both knew they were competing for the same budget dollars and their pet projects were comparable in terms of their value to the company. The first manager got up and methodically went through the key points of his project. All the immediate questions were answered. The next manager addressed the group but something was very different. There was an elevated level of enthusiasm. She conveyed a personal passion and commitment that was apparent in her voice and her body language supported the spoken message. Guess who won? Be passionate about your message. Think it's just a senior staff briefing or a lifelong customer? It doesn't matter. The thing to remember, however, is that passion comes "from within– not from outside." It can rarely be convincingly manufactured. Has it been a while since you were passionate about those things in your presentations?

The Eye Contact:
"And the dragon flew in front of them, stopped, turned and looked them right in the eye!"

Those who tell stories to kids in the libraries or street fairs are masters of eye contact. Watch them. Watch their eyes watching their audience's eyes. They connect for only a moment, but they work the young audience to make sure that every person in the room is hanging onto every word. Watch the problem youngster in the front row. The storyteller will hold that eye contact a moment or two longer and will occasionally take a small step or two towards the youngster. This subtle movement often brings the youngster back into the story. **The slight invasion of his/her "personal space" makes it difficult to disregard the storyteller.** Ever had someone nod off or appear to be disinterested in your presentation? This happens to the best of us, but this simple technique can help you regain the audience's attention. Eye contact and body position can help keep your audience more closely involved with what you have to say.

The Close:
"The village was saved, the dragon went home to live with his family, and life got back to normal in the small village of Newbergia."

Ok, so business stories don't all have happy endings, but they do need to end. Far too often presentations come to an anti-climatic close leaving audiences wondering if you're done or if you simply ran out of slides. What do you want your audience to do with the information you just gave them? Take action? Decide favorably for your project proposal? Buy your product or service? When you close a presentation, never leave your audience wondering. If you've told your stories well, they will want to take action; we do the audience a disservice by not telling them how. Even motivational speakers will conclude with the one or two things for the audience to remember. That's because those who speak for a living understand the value of the close. It's time to think about how you conclude your presentations.

Next time you're cruising the Internet, check out a few web sites that deal with the art of storytelling (search under "storyteller"). You will discover a fascinating parallel to the art of presenting. It's easy to forget that every presentation has a story to tell. What's yours? Successful storytelling may not get you that next big raise, but these important enhancements in the way you present will clearly make your life slightly more "happier ever after."

Shrink Wrap
Dr. Scott Lee

Personal stories: Your most powerful presentation tool

"Did you hear the one about the bartender and the priest," begins a presenter at a recent seminar I attended. Stories catch our attention immediately due to the nature of the material; it is right-brain intensive and we generally find that material refreshing (sensory, images, graphics, feeling, experiential, creative, etc.).

This presenter had the right idea. Begin the presentation with something memorable, preferably a story. But he limited the audience's response and, therefore, limited their ability to engage in his presentation.

His story was simply a joke and, as such, entertained but did not connect meaningfully with the audience. It dealt with a make-believe situation instead of grounding his presentation introduction in reality. It created an expectation of entertainment rather than learning.

Contrast such a joke with an opening that might begin with the words, "Yesterday, I had one of those heart-pounding, white-knuckle experiences…." Why are we more drawn to this latter story? I believe that we are basically relational and curious beings. At my office, the waiting room is filled with numerous magazines. While clients could be reading US News, the Atlantic Monthly, or various boating journals, clearly the magazine most read is People. Why? We are curious. People magazine writes good stories, and these stories are about real people. We are interested in real experiences, especially if the rich and famous struggle with similar experiences as we do. **Personal stories connect meaningfully with the audience because they engage the audience with the presenter in the common ground of personal experience**.

Furthermore, as personal stories open the world of the presenter to the audience, the credibility of the presenter is enhanced. However, it is important that the personal story is believable. Significant events impress an audience, but far-fetched miracles are difficult to buy. Personal stories create a sense of vulnerability when they are from someone we respect, which allows us as the audience to feel comfortable and to be interested in what the presenter has to say.

When presentations take a turn for the worse, when something unexpected happens, or if you hear snoring from the audience, then a personal story can help reconnect you with the audience.

A personal story engages the curiosity of the audience. It enhances credibility by showing that you have life experiences. It activates the right brain where you wake up and remember your own common experiences. Notice events in your life, understand common threads, and write these on index cards as personal stories for illustrating your presentation messages. Before long, you will notice that personal stories are a daily happening and illustrations are everywhere around you. Be ready to use them in a pinch. Personal stories have been connecting with audiences for thousands of years and they continue to be one of our most effective communication tools.

Survival Summaries
TIPS for storytelling in presentations

- Make your stories **personal** by relating your own unique experiences. There's no substitute for relating relevant and believable personal stories.

- Make them **relevant** by creating clear verbal connections back to your point. Stories that seem to fill time but have little connectivity are perceived as time fillers.

- Make them relatively **short** so the point doesn't get lost in the journey. If your story takes longer than just a few minutes to tell well, decide whether it's worth telling at all. The longer the story, the more opportunity for you to get off track or forget details that make it work.

- Make them **polished and practiced** so they're told conversationally. The point of storytelling can be unraveled if the delivery is mechanical.

- Use them **strategically** at the beginning and closing of a presentation. Creating presentation "bookends" with good theme connectivity can be a powerful presentation memory trigger tool for your audience.

- **Don't confuse** joke telling with storytelling. Not only are jokes harder to relate to a topic, audiences will have little patience for a badly told joke. However, they do flex in their willingness to go along with a personal story.

Survival Skill 4

Craft the Images

Any good presentation is a carefully orchestrated balance of elements. Dynamic delivery skills without solid presentation content and graphics is like eating Chinese food. It quickly fills you up but leaves you hungry a short time later. Likewise, the laptop computer and electronic projector that just cost your company a bundle is still capable of projecting embarrassingly amateur content.

A well-illustrated story is essential to communicating a memorable presentation message. Although many professional speakers can prevail with the sheer power of their delivery skills, most presenters today simply need more. The more facets a message might have, the higher the requirement to display and build visual reinforcement to the spoken word. Never have relevant photos, illustrations and artwork been as mission-critical to the process. Unfortunately, presenters are often turning to the wrong sources for presentation graphics imagery. Survival Skill #4 offers up some guidance on presentation graphics and design.

Templates
The frame that sets off your presentation content.

Base artwork
The nuts and bolts of presentation images.

Animation
How object movement can be meaningful once again.

Fonts
What every presenter should know about fonts.

Color
Applying common sense criteria to color usage.

Sound and video
Leverage these dimensional elements to drive higher retention.

Managing a collaborative presentation effort
Assembling content from many sources.

"There is a deep desire within the consciousness of man to create something better today than yesterday's best."

– John Orr Young

A Closer look...
Templates

Shaping the frame that encompasses your presentation content.

Corporate marketing identity

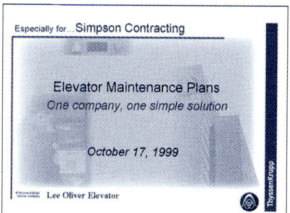

Marketing departments are given the responsibility of creating and shaping the image of a company. This activity extends to all forms of communication. Literally tens of thousands of dollars are invested in this process. Amidst the brochures, annual reports, display ads and datasheets, there's one tool that's more personal, more media rich and is used at the most critical times in the sales process than all the others: the business presentation. Yet, despite its essential role, well-defined marketing communication standards are frequently overlooked in those presentations tools, allowing overworked administrative assistants and travel-weary executives to take control of the process start to finish.

Make sure your template leverages these important business identity elements:

- Appropriate use of logo color, size and placement.
- Colors consistent with other corporate usage standards.
- Utilize corporate sanctioned fonts as long as it doesn't compromise readability. Also, font

embedding is not an exact science and can add much file size to a presentation file.

- Identity images or illustrations used frequently in other corporate communication tools can bring a unique look and continuity to the corporate presentation template while providing linkage of company identity.

A common corporate template that pre-selects fonts, placement, appropriate colors and sanctioned look and feel creates a unique and professional standard for all company presenters.

Ease of assembly of presentations from many sources

The value in a common corporate template extends well beyond just the look. If you've ever tried to assemble a single presentation with slides provided from a number of different presenters using different templates, you've probably had a mess on your hands. Copy/pasting between slide sorters creates problems requiring text resizing, moving of graphics and frustrating line-wrapping issues. It's rarely as easy as copy-paste unless your company has standardized on one single presentation template. Although not the total answer, a common template can shave hours off the process of presentation content collaboration. (More to come on this topic later in the Survival Guide.)

Base artwork

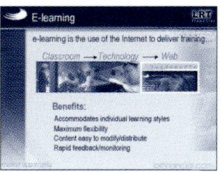

The nuts and bolts of presentation images.

This step is where many presentations go badly wrong. Your sense of the appropriate when it comes to presentations is often driven by what you see other presenters deliver. If you were writing a novel, you wouldn't be looking for inspiration in a comic book. When it comes to professional and appropriate presentation content, your aim should be set much higher than the usual presentations. Average should be a dirty word for your company.

Leverage text information correctly:

Try to stick to five or six bullets per slide. No more than one line per bullet if possible. Don't use periods. Try to avoid text only without some reinforcing support graphic.

Avoid cases where single words wrap to a second line (orphans).

Charts tell their own stories:

Remember, charts are primarily for illustrating trends and creating impressions, nothing more, nothing less. The very best charts are the simplest ones.

Skill #4 – Craft the Images

They use relevant visual imagery to create interesting "perspectives" on the data. Try to plot the sum total of all knowledge and watch your audience's eyes glaze over. Demonstrate through your charts what's really important. Keep them simple and stage the information through the use of animation builds.

Illustrations embellish text:

As we've discussed, sensory-based information is cognitively processed much differently than traditional text-based content. For that reason you should always be seeking ways of converting words to images. Even when building basic graphical elements like boxes or circles, try to think of ways of making them more interesting. Apply a related picture to the front of the box or use shading that implies dimension. Good artwork exists out there if you look, so don't fall into the clip art trap!

We live in a visually–oriented world; five-second sound bits, 30-second television commercials, and television dramas that miraculously create complete closure every 30 to 60 minutes. If your audience wants to read something, they'll go buy a good book. The last place they want to be reading a bunch of material is in a presentation. Just as dramatic motion pictures have the need to integrate occasional comic relief to make the drama that much more compelling, so your presentations need to seek out ways to add graphical relief on a regular basis so that the text you use carries more impact. It makes the presentation tighter and more information-packed.

Using graphical, non-text approaches to telling your story is an intentional act. It doesn't happen accidentally and requires some planning and thought. Here are some ideas to jog your creative juices the next time you put together a big presentation.

Clip art

Although appropriate for informal settings, familiar clip art images like those found in presentation software will convey a pronounced informality and light-hearted atmosphere to the venue. Don't take the easy way out with these elements. Informal images can transcend the medium and connect with the audience but must be chosen carefully.

Optimizing scanned images

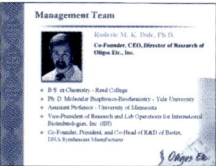

It's easy enough these days to scan up a few images to use in your presentation, but be sure they're clean, well-composed and optimized for the presentation medium you've chosen. If the images can't be clean, you're better off not using them.

Avoid the "brick." That's how network administrators refer to those huge graphic files that are passed around, duplicated and stored on their valuable network resources. If the scanned images for your presentations have created huge presentation files, this message is for you. Optimize those scanned image files so they're no larger than what they truly need to be for your chosen presentation medium. Follow these guidelines for smaller scanned image file sizes.

Scanning guidelines for bitmap images in presentations

Medium	DPI	Scaling	Color Depth	Format
35mm slides	200-250	Close to import size	24-bit	JPEG
Overheads	300	Close to import size	24-bit	JPEG
Electronics	72	Close to import size	24-bit	JPEG
Web Pres.	72	Close to import size	8-bit	JPEG/GIF

Note: *Graphics that are optimized down for lower resolution mediums cannot be successfully "rez'ed" (increase DPI resolution) back up for higher resolution requirements so be sure to archive the high resolution images.*

Color depth

There are many attributes to the presentation images you use. We've just discussed resolution, but now let's introduce another. Color depth is the amount of unique colors an individual pixel can choose from in displaying an image. You may have heard these terms before, now let's define them:

1-bit	1 color	Black and white images
8-bit	256 colors	Color or gray scale images
16-bit	65,500 colors	Color images
24-bit	16.8 million colors	Color images

Stock photo libraries

While we're on the subject of bitmap images, stock photography libraries are widely available online or on CD ROM. They can provide your presentation with just the right touch of realism to augment your topic. Read the license agreements closely to understand usage guidelines and optimize the images as indicated earlier in this chapter. Just like any libraries, some images are better than others so be discerning. One of the most comprehensive of the online image sites is **www.gettyworks.com** where in addition to a vast image library you'll also discover a section of the site dealing specifically with presentation-related issues and ideas.

Tip #1 Consider your resolution requirements. If the graphics will only be used in electronic presentation purchase low (screen)-resolution images and save a lot.

Tip #2 It would be more cost-effective to purchase 100 topic-related images on a CD ROM rather than paying for individual images online.

Tip #3 As your archive of stock images increases , consider using a software utility like Extensis' Portfolio to categorize and search your images quickly. It takes time to set up initially but in the long run, you'll be doing yourself a favor.

Animation

How object movement can be meaningful once again.

➡ *The seven-second rule:*

Presentation animations have run amok ever since presenters discovered the freedom to make things move. The idea that "it ain't groov'in unless it's mov'in" was funny at first but has now become the electronic presentation equivalent of fingernails on a blackboard. It's one thing to try to upgrade your graphics, it's quite another to give them motion sickness.

The best application of movement in a presentation is for the chunking and staging of more visually complex information.

46 Skill #4 – Craft the Images

Overly complex screen content is commonplace so try this approach. Apply the seven-second rule at every opportunity. If someone who's never seen your presentation can't figure out the basic theme of your information in seven seconds, it's time to unpack it into more bit-sized chunks of data and visual elements. Logically group topic elements and introduce them on a mouse-click.

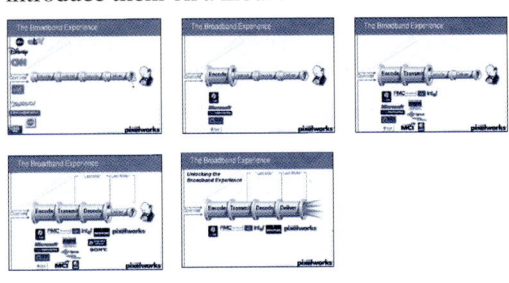

You get the opportunity to verbally build the concept while your audience absorbs the complete information slowly. Everybody wins and you exit the presentation with more dignity than if you turned it into an animation circus sideshow.

Fonts
What every presenter should know about fonts

It seems like fonts have become the sampler tray in the window of the presentation candy shop. You get freebees with software applications and it seems like you can purchase a billion on a CD for a mere $49.95. Every time you open a document with embedded fonts, your list of choices continues to grow on your computer. Lest you get too giddy with the use of fonts in your next presentation, let's look at this unique venue of presentation graphics and the downside to unrestrained font embedding.

Purpose behind font usage

For most marketing communication tools (brochures, display ads), fonts are carefully chosen to be compliant with the company's graphical standards. Because the resolution of those pieces are relatively high, a tasteful and consistent font treatment can create a seamless extension to the company "look."

Considerations for use in electronic presentations:

- **Readability**

Having said that, some fonts that look great in a brochure simply won't work in a presentation. As a matter of fact, they won't be readable at all, which should be your primary concern in the lower resolution world of electronic presentations. All the company standards in the world will miss the mark if your message can't be read. Add to that a standard presentation drop shadow treatment on a narrow or serif font face and the perceived double image will have your audience crossing their eyes.

- **Font embedding**

There's a cost to font embedding as well. Recently I had a 300k PowerPoint presentation that used just a few different fonts. When I embedded the fonts (PowerPoint 97 – File, Save As "with fonts" or PowerPoint 2000 Save As, Tools Menu), the file size jumped up to a whopping 3.1MB. So, what's it worth to you to port around the extra file size to support your fonts? Lest you think this is an exact science, it's not. Some fonts that have appeared to embed correctly do not. This initiates a call from the person on the other end of your email describing strange line wraps and character spacing. Simply choosing from the stock selection of available Windows fonts will ensure you're supported without embedding.

There's a place for embedded fonts. Just understand the trade-offs and the ultimate reason we use them, i.e.: to communicate information and to be clearly understood with as little text as necessary. Some fonts are more readable than others but fall into these two basic categories.

san serif   serif

Most graphic design teams understand the power of fontography (the selection and use of font faces and families to translate moods and impressions). They can convey a professional elegance or a playful informality. They can be clear and legible at their very best or, at their worst, frustrate an audience because they're simply not readable (i.e., wide drop shadows on a Times Roman). Just because you can embed fonts does not necessarily mean you should.

Color

Any reasonable discussion about presentation graphics should include something about the use of color. To many business presenters, color represents a near infinite pallet of opportunity to make a presentation more visually interesting. To a graphic artist, color is a carefully orchestrated design component that can carry powerful subliminal messages. One thing we can say for sure, it's easy to abuse color. PowerPoint has tried to provide some guidance with pre-created templates - all with specifically defined color schemes. (Format-Slide Color Scheme).

To those with little art background, the ability to spot colors that don't work well together may not be very refined. In some settings, bright, loud colors can put off an audience. In other settings, weaker pastel colors can create a less powerful impression. Here are a couple of tips to help you put some sanity back into the color picking process.

Tip#1 Take your lead from your marketing departments and their recommended use of color. This will also create some visual continuity within your company.

Tip#2 Have someone outside of your presentation process do a sanity check on the colors you've selected. A little honesty at this point may save you some embarrassment later.

Tip#3 Remember, less is usually more. Select your primary 8 colors in the Color Scheme menu and stick with them throughout the presentation.

For more information on the impact of color, check out **www.colormatters.com**. You'll never look at color the same way again.

Sound and video

Digital sound & video are now much easier to integrate and can make your presentations much more memorable.

Skill #4 – Craft the Images

Sound files

Presentation sound can become an elegant sensory-based reinforcement to your key presentation messages or it can turn your presentation into a multimedia zoo through the inappropriate use of audible reinforcement. Screeching tires, lasers and typewriter sounds are best left for those fun, informal internal presentations and then only used once.

Your audience and the level of informality will always drive these issues, but here are a few other ideas for including meaningful sound elements:

- **Music:** Short music cuts are better than music that's continuously playing during the presentation. Extended music is a distraction that you do not need. Keep the music topic-related while matching the "flavor" and context of the meeting. Copyright issues should always be a consideration when using music. Unless you or a friend wrote the lick, someone, somewhere owns the copyright. Written approvals are required and occasionally granted but not without some exchange of cash, attribution or both.

- **Sound effects:** Most sound effects come across as a gratuitous attempt at filling time and space because some presenters don't have the real "beef" in their presentations. However, if the sound effects can introduce a touch of reality using the senses, it can be very dramatic and engaging. For example, a client of mine was one of the largest elevator maintenance companies in the country. They used the sound associated with an elevator starting and stopping during slide transitions between major topic areas in the presentation. It worked well.

Another example might be the noises associated with the trading floor of the stock market used at strategic parts of a financial services presentation.

TIPS on the use of sound effects

- Keep them short.
- Don't use them too frequently.
- Be creative.
- Avoid stock sounds in your presentation software.

▸ **Voice-over:** Perhaps one of the most effective applications of a presentation sound element would be in the use of an industry expert, your CEO, a celebrity or other type of voice to add a sensory-based dimension to your text and images. Bringing others into your presentations to reinforce key messages is much more effective than the audience simply getting your well-rehearsed perspective.

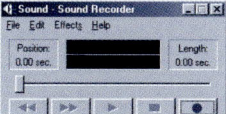

Creating those files can be as simple as plugging your cassette tape player into the microphone or AUX-in port on your sound card and using the Windows Sound Recorder (Start-Programs-Accessories-Entertainment-Sound Recorder) to convert the analog tape file into a computer digital file.

▸ **Video clips:** Whether you're trying to leverage analog video played back from your VCR or a brief digitized video clip that's been embedded into your presentation, the impact can be dramatic. The "change-up" from the existing flow of the presentation immediately re-engages audiences. Its strong sensory-based nature can elevate the impact of the entire presentation when those video elements are judiciously included. Important things to consider when using digital video are:

- If the digital video segment is longer than 50-70 seconds, consider sticking with the original analog videotape. It's easy enough these days toggling between computer and video sources on your electronic projector and it eliminates computer file size concerns, plus you get a full screen image.

- A great application of video might include industry experts and corporate executives, taking your audience to a place that relates to your presentation, or perhaps just an interesting segue between topics.

- Computers with greater RAM tend to play back digital video with superior performance over faster computers with more limited RAM.

- Be sure your PC supports the CODEC (digital video compression approach) that was used for the digital video file. You can check installed Windows CODECs by visiting START - Settings - Control Panel - Multimedia - Devices Tab - Video Compression CODECS. Mpeg video is great with its 100+:1 compression ratios but is not as universally supported as other digital video formats.

Shrink Wrap
Dr. Scott Lee
Armegedon and technology

It was 3:00 a.m. and I was certain that Gabriel's trumpets would not have been as loud as the rumblings I heard that first night from the freshman dorm of Wheaton College. Nobody had told me about the train tracks when they recruited me to Wheaton. They ran so close to the dorm that I was convinced the end was near each time I was awakened with the shaking of my bed by the passing Union Pacific. And in the morning, I was joined by 450 other bleary-eyed frosh who also experienced an unforgettable night of startled reflexes mixed with brief episodes of sleep.

Yet just as significant as that surprise jostling on my first night in the dorm was the ability to sleep undisturbed after about three weeks, completely oblivious to the passing trains and their blasting (or was that "blasted") whistles. We all began to return to life as usual about the time of our first midterms, and it was at that time that I began to understand the powerful message of **habituation**. While the trains were just as obnoxiously loud as before, the brain effectively screened out this noise and therefore no train noise was perceived. **I learned that any continuous, patterned stimulation that is not meaningful to us is screened-out as non-significant, background noise.** We get used to it and then we don't notice the sound because it is meaningless to us at that time.

Our brains love stimulation and the adventure of something new. But when we listen to presenters who do not vary their presentations in pace or tone, failing to add graphics or stories, we call them "monotonous" and we tune these presentations out. We stop listening to their "points" and our minds wander to something more interesting… Equally boring can become the presentation where multiple technical elements such as sound effects are used so much so that they are considered by our brains to be non-significant background noise and we tune this out as well. In the same way as using too many spices spoil the dinner, too many special effects lose their effectiveness and get lost in the onslaught of flying bullets and spinning words.

To minimize the impact of habituation with our audiences, be sure to occasionally pause or vary the pace of the presentation. Spice the delivery with appropriate graphics and story material to vary the mental processing of the audience but be sure your spice adds to the flavor rather than drowning out the flavor of your presentation. Bringing something new to your message—such as a personal story, a recent news account, a relevant video clip—will keep your message fresh in the minds of your audience and out of the realm of meaningless background noise.

Managing a collaborative presentation effort...

Nowadays there's a whole lot of collaboration that goes into most presentations. The CFO or finance department has some charts they want to include. The Sales Manager incessantly wordsmiths each phrase until it has just the right ring. And then, there's the CEO. If it's a smaller company, s/he wants to get in his/her two cents worth. The good news is you're not lacking for sources of input The challenge is that often the end result is a patchwork quilt of graphics, text treatments, colors and composition. Here are some essential tips to help your next collaborative effort go more smoothly:

Tip #1: Work from a standardized template...
Creating continuity in collaboration

If you've seen the movie Titanic, it's pretty tough not to be overwhelmed with the visual magnitude of everything your eyes were absorbing. It's mind boggling to say the least. From expansive shipyard panoramas to the decadent interiors, you found yourself drawn deeply into the era. I remember the first time I saw it: three hours (and my jumbo tub of popcorn) later, I realized the director never once betrayed the fact that much of what I saw was created from the minds of some very creative computer graphic artists. Now, for a moment, I want you to imagine that halfway through the movie the camera slowly panned across the top deck with Jack and Rose talking in the foreground. Suddenly, you become aware of a seam in the backdrop or, better yet, the computer artist decided she wanted to airbrush in the Statue of Liberty coming up out of the North Atlantic background (she just got bored making water, I guess). Nothing bursts the bubble of expectation quicker than when you get caught up in an experience only to find that things are not what they appeared to be.

Often, you see both large and small companies alike invest huge amounts of money in image creation. Saturn, "a different kind of car company," or Allstate, "the good hands people." All those millions of marketing dollars for ads, brochures and websites, spent for one purpose - to get you to

Skill #4 – Craft the Images

believe certain things about a company through the use of images and words.

Just like the hypothetical "bored artist" took some liberty with the movie, thousands of times **every day sales people and corporate executives get in front of major customers, partners and peers with presentations and supporting graphics that bear no resemblance to their corporate identities**.

The colors, font rules, supporting images and key messaging that were so carefully crafted are all jettisoned for the presentation. At a time where the final impression could mean thousands or millions of dollars, someone took the presentation into their own hands. What's wrong with this picture?

- Have your marketing department provide standards for colors, logo usage and supporting images.

- Backgrounds created with paint programs (i.e., PhotoShop) far extend the capabilities available in your presentation software for design and elegance.

- Font support: First priority: readability; second priority: corporate standards.

- Set up all appropriate colors in the Color Scheme menus so others can make good choices.

- In slide Master(s), properly align text fields and allow for a two-line title wrap if it occurs.

- Create several sample slides for template users that reinforce good rules (i.e., five bullets per slide).

- A good job of initial setup means slides can be added later without timely reformatting.
- In PowerPoint 2000, some corporate standards for bullet usage, capitalization rules other styles can be set into your presentation. Those departing from those standards will get a friendly reminder. (Tools – Options – Spelling and Style)

Tip #2: Determine the gatekeeper for standardization

The only way to ensure that your presentation collaboration effort doesn't turn into a smorgasbord of punctuation, font usage, capitalization and a formatting circus is to appoint someone who'll watch out for such mundane but visually essential details. Don't think it's a problem? Watch the next few presentations you sit through and observe how the rules related to formatting will constantly change. Here's what your standards gatekeeper will need to watch for:

Capitalization rules are closely followed

- **Titles:** All title slides should exhibit an identical capitalization treatment. Avoid all caps. Like email etiquette, all caps SHOUT in your audience's face.

- **Body text:** All bullets should be consistent in style. The exceptions are proper names and words like "and", "the", "or", "for". Remember, no periods at the end of bullets. It implies that they are sentences to be read, not succinct information to be scanned.

- **Labels:** Labels permeate most presentations on charts, boxes, graphs and photographs. Set the rules for capitalization, size and make sure they're followed.

Tip #3: Provide a message continuity review

Before the final presentation effort is put to rest, provide a collaborative critique session for all those involved. Lay down the ground rules about what is and is not negotiable and how the presentation is to be distributed. Project the images on screen and get consensus on all issues. Trying to get final buy-off from others outside that meeting will only lengthen the approval process. If your presentation team is remotely located, this might be a great opportunity to post the presentation on a free web conferencing service such as (**www.myplaceware.com**) for a group critique and final review.

Be aware that build slides are not supported by all browser types so they will need to be manually created as consecutive slides for web-based presentations.

Shrink Wrap
Dr. Scott Lee
ADHD and Technology

I just finished returning my messages that came in today while I was in therapy sessions. One call was from an exasperated mother. She said, "I have an 11 y/o son who won't sit still, he doesn't listen to me or his teachers, and I think we're losing him. I need some help." I receive calls like this every week, and the medical community refers to this type of difficulty as ADHD (Attention Deficit Hyperactivity Disorder). This type of client has difficulty focusing on multiple stimuli or attending for any period of time.

Our presentation audiences are not very different from "ADHD" clients. They want to pay attention but are easily distracted. When presented with too many stimuli (i.e. multiple slides, lots of bullets, many background colors or complex graphics, etc.) the listener tunes out, fading away to another place in his mind.

We treat the ADHD client by first limiting the stimuli (decreasing the distractions, such as sit the student in the front row, not behind chatty peers). Second, it is very important to keep the message clear (repeating the main point and providing one-step directions rather than complex procedures to follow). A third approach is to teach the client to relax and use sensory awareness to engage this person experientially.

Each of these approaches also helps presenters when addressing "attention- challenged" audiences—which includes most of them. For all the great achievements and spellbinding power of technology, too much is still too much. Use your technology wisely, appropriate to your message. It is to illustrate and restate your message, not take the place of it.

Survival Summaries

- **The first critical impression**

    The presentation template is not an after thought. Rather, it's the first critical impression an audience sees. Make it count.

- **Bulleted information**

    Keep bulleted information succinct. It should be non-sentences and phrases limited to five or six one-line statements per screen. Avoid cases where single words wrap to a second line (orphans).

Skill #4 – Craft the Images

- **Charts**

  Charts are rarely intended for their detail. Create impressions, define trends and keep them simple with relevant and interesting imagery. Animate them to compliment your "story."

- **Graphics**

  Choose your graphics carefully. Professional caliber presentations need to be supported with professional-quality graphics.

- **Good collaboration in presentation development includes these considerations:**
  - Work from a company standard template.
  - Appoint a standards gatekeeper to create consistency in capitalization rules, alignment, color & font usage.
  - Provide a final presentation review with all contributors to ensure continuity of message.

Case Study

While working with a group of presentation designers, I provided several of them with multi-colored containers of children's clay. The only instructions were, "create something you saw at your last picnic." When I came back to them later they had molded 3 very different concepts ranging from ants on a blanket to a swing set. Same instructions – 3 uniquely different outcomes. Merging our "mental models" of what the outcome of our presentations should look like is an important first step when starting the project. If we don't, someone will be disappointed.

Survival Skill 5

Gain the Mental Presentation Edge

It's not enough these days to be physically up to a task. Ask any good golfer, tennis player, baseball pitcher or even a CEO trying to raise another half million dollars in bridge capital. The mental part of the "game" can become a much more significant factor than just being physically ready to push mouse buttons. The next time you're prepping for a big presentation, don't forget to get your mind as ready for the big presentation day as your laptop presentation. That means mental crispness and the ability to handle the unexpected issues that arise during a big presentation.

Envisioning success
Being mentally ready takes preparation.

Dealing with presentation fear
Manage the beast within.

When you go blank
Quick recovery techniques.

The "two-minute drill" for presenters
What to do when your presentation time is cut short.

"Experience is not what happens to you, it is what you do with what happens to you."
– Aldous Huxley

A Closer Look...
The perfect presentation day!

For some presenters, the idea of perfection and presentations is an oxymoron, and they're right. There's no such thing as a perfect presentation or perfect presenters. Even those who are very polished presenters scrutinize their best efforts for what they could have done differently. They are always their toughest critics!

For others, the negative memories of presentations gone wrong continue to haunt them and impair even their best preparation efforts. They anticipate technology mishaps, cold non-responsive audiences, and low presentation energy. They start to anticipate failure long before the day ever comes. Psychologists tell us that unless we reprogram those possible outcomes in our minds, we will fulfill them time and time again.

If this sounds like you, find a quiet spot, sit back in your chair and get comfortable, because we're going to walk through the perfect presentation day. Revisiting this positive outcome exercise on a regular basis and prior to presentations can change old patterns of presenting and reinforce positive anticipation of the process.

It's the morning before the big presentation...

and you're sitting at the breakfast table. You're relaxed because you're totally prepared for today's presentation. As the sun streams in the window and you feel its warmth on your skin, you're actually getting excited for the day's events. You can already imagine an audience that is as excited to hear what you have to say as you are to say it.

On the drive in, you find that the anxiety attack you normally experience has been replaced with a strong feeling of well being, a quiet confidence in the fact that you're ready and it's actually going to be fun.

As you arrive at the meeting room, the early arrivers are already there and there's an excited buzz in the room. You can overhear some of the comments as you walk through the crowd. "I've heard good things about this presentation." "A friend of mine heard her (or him) a while back and said she (or he) was really well worth hearing!"

Your laptop and projector are quickly set up and your title slide is waiting patiently on screen. No surprises because you've anticipated every potential challenge and practiced what you would do. The only thing remaining is the fun of looking into those expectant faces and delivering the presentation of your life. Sure, there will be a few sour faces but you feel sorry for them, not for yourself. You see, it will take them a bit longer to get caught up in your presentation then the rest. They're the ones who will miss out.

Skill #5 – Gain the Mental Presentation Edge

As you wait off to the side during the introduction, you can sense a very positive, affirming anticipation.

The smiles on the faces you see remind you that the audience also wants you to succeed.

The room erupts in applause as you step up to the podium. The warmth in the room is electric. As you speak, you notice that the audience is attentive to every word. Your eye contact with those in the room is met with positive nods and smiles. Your presentation graphics are just the right balance of support and substance to keep the audience constantly coming back to you. This is actually quite fun!

At the conclusion of your presentation, the audience breaks into warm applause. Attendees come up to you, shake your hand and thank you for coming. You truly gave them a gift today, something they will remember. You have the confidence to take on bigger and tougher audiences because you've come to realize that it's about your personal best efforts, not just the mood of your audience. Good presentation skills emerge from the confidence that what you will contribute that day is worthwhile and important. Congratulations! This is the first day of the rest of your presentation life.

Just psycho babble?

Perhaps you're a bit skeptical. That's good. You should be. But for those who've been paralyzed by past experiences, good intentions for better presenting are rarely enough. Your mind can be either a powerful ally in what you bring into the presentation or a nemesis that is constantly reminding you of failure. If a little personal affirmation and reinforcement can give you back just a little bit of the edge, it's well worth the effort.

Shrink Wrap
Dr. Scott Lee
How to Deal with Presention Fear
Managing the "beast" within

Fear, to varying degrees, is a common experience for most presenters. For a few, it's not simply a distraction but an overwhelming detriment to their personal success and they feel powerless to do anything about it. Take heart, there aresome steps available to help you manage your passion. I say passion because the body is experiencing the same physiological experience when anxious as it does when excited or even aroused. The body doesn't understand this as negative until the mind labels your experience in that way. You might be having a better time than you thought!

I was speaking to couples on marriage issues at a local conference ground when the entire back of the auditorium cleared out, row by row, and I figured I would quit the speaking circuit right then.

Later, I found out there was a small fire in an adjoining building and they were carefully emptying the auditorium out of caution, trying not to alarm anyone. Too bad no one thought to mention it to me.

Fear is not always a bad thing. We should be fearful about some things: jumping out of airplanes without a parachute, sliding off cliffs, or not paying our income taxes for the third straight year. But sometimes fear takes over when it doesn't need to.

To moderate our anxiety and calm the beast within, we must know a little about anxiety.

Anxiety is the opposite of feeling relaxed, they cannot coexist. Anxiety is based on fear of the unknown and is found most often when we feel things are unpredictable, not knowing what will come next. I know that I was anxious on most first dates, when auditioning for drama parts, and when playing in youth summer baseball tournaments out of state. The personal stakes were high and my performance was uncertain. To counter such anxiety, the best approaches are:

1) Cognitive: imagination and planning, and

2) Physiological: learning to relax the body.

These may seem like big concepts but they're pretty straight-forward.

➡ Tip #1: Mental preparation

Thoughts that help to moderate fear are those that create alternate personal experiences of enjoyment or humor instead of the dark, painful expectations of all gone wrong. Therefore, take control and level your playing field mentally. Instead of seeing the audience as all-powerful know-it-alls who should be presenting instead of you, use the **right brain** to see them as five year-old kindergarten kids who eagerly await anything their teacher says. Notice the clothes they would be wearing, how their faces would look, etc.

Alternatively, forget about the audience and remember a wonderful experience in a sensory-filled environment and recreate that experience in detail. A vacation on a warm, white California beach, a cabin in the snow with a roaring, colorful fire, sitting in the bubbly jacuzzi all can serve as the focus of your attention and take over your senses. Notice the colors, movement, warmth, sounds, smells, etc. that fill your experience. We quickly and deeply relate to our stored exerperiences.

How'd that go? Well, the better (more detail) you remember and recreate your own personal experience, the more relaxed and comfortable you will feel.

I guarantee it, because you are engaging the right brain almost exclusively and your fear is almost all left brain.

You may want to reference that again in Survival Skill #3.

The **left brain** can be helpful in this process as well. Because presentation fear is usually based upon the unknown and unpredictable, let's get big-time predictable. The opposite of unpredictable is structure, structure, structure. This means clear and careful planning of your presentation, memorized stories to be told at specific intervals, taking drinks of water during certain planned slides, and lots of practice.

There is no replacement for preparation when it comes to utilizing the left brain to fight fear. Although you may come across as more stiff than you would like, you will begin to get your track record of positive presentations established. Then, you can return to the "game day approach" described previously.

► Tip #2: Physical workout

It is also possible to decrease the fear component through physiological means. Since the body has activated the sympathetic portion of the autonomic nervous system (you know, the "fight or flight" stuff when you're pretty wired), the body wants to get physical; specifically, sweat. Twenty minutes of sweat will calm the body. The point is to do the sweating before the presentation, not during. Taking a brisk walk the morning of your presentation will help; a hot soak in the Jacuzzi or even a long, hot, shower will also create relaxed muscles. And when your muscles relax, your brain moves in concert to join your body.

What to do when you go blank
Quick recovery ideas

I had a friend who wrote his entire Master's thesis on the computer, without ever powering down, believing that he wouldn't need to save his work as long as the computer stayed on. He was, of course, correct; but he didn't account for that power outage. Our minds can act similarly.

One spark in the wrong direction, an alarm in your environment, an attractive person smiling in the third row, a sudden appearance of something unexpected, and your mind goes blank.

I mean really blank, as in not remembering where you are for a moment, what you are doing, or whom you are addressing. The save function has failed you; there is no helpful cue and you are, for the moment, a deer caught in the headlights. If this has happened to you, you know that you need a plan. If this has not happened to you, it probably will. You still need a plan.

Case Study
A note from Scott...

I try to integrate movie clips into my presentations whenever possible; others "get it" much more quickly when connecting with clips they have seen. For one presentation to about 600 high school juniors and seniors, I set up four clips; but since I like the clips to reinforce the points already made, I was working hard to establish my points. I was so focused on making the fourth point that I began to add stories to draw out the point further. I became so engrossed in these great stories (which I had not planned to use) that I got lost in the story and forgot the point. My body responded with fight or flight and I couldn't recall how I was going to finish the talk. My left-brain confusion was taking over. **The eyes of my audience became glazed over and I thought my speaking career was about finished**. So, I fell back on old reliable: play the final video clip.

Raiders of the Lost Ark: The Last Crusade was the clip, and was I ever glad to see it. First, it gave me a three-minute break to gather myself. Second, it was all right-brain material; the point I was trying to make connected immediately. Third, it was a darn good clip (about letting go of the challis when it would cost you your life). I remember, the audience "got it," and the close was easy. Whew.

There are several ways to respond when you go blank; because a lot of them are not pretty, it is critical to plan ahead. It is important to use cues to keep your path clear as you traverse your presentation.

➡ Tip #1: Remember the topics in a presentation like rooms in a house

One of the oldest memory devices is to imagine that you are walking through a house, placing one idea in each room. Perhaps in the entryway you place your opening story about Fido saving your kid from the big green frog. In the living room you have your first point, "Dogs are man's best friend through the ages." The kitchen might keep the next point, "Care for dogs includes healthy food choices," and the bedroom might be host to, "Why Fido curls on your bed at night." Your conclusion might be placed in the basement, attic, back porch, etc, where you conclude, "Dogs are what make us most human." To keep from getting lost in this presentation, just try to remember where you were last in the house.

➡ Tip #2: Move to illustrations that trigger a train of rehearsed thought

Following the illustrations provides another type of mental support as in the case study above. If you have four key slides, three key video clips, or special stories, then they must be organized before the presentation; they then can be used to pull you back to your topic. If you are lost, there is a VERY good chance that your audience is also. Since audiences want to be found, not lost, they will be very happy if you just move along in your presentation to something that will cue everybody in on where this presentation is going. While it is nice to be able to set up your graphic illustrations with appropriate content, it is absolutely fine to use the graphic illustrations to lead you to your content as well.

➡ Tip #3: Integrate subtle key words into your presentation screens

At the bottom of each presentation page, create visual clues that represent the different topic areas represented in your agenda. Those agenda items can be indicated as a single subtle word across the screen bottom. Use a subdued color for those non-current topics and highlight the specific topic you're addressing. In addition to getting you back on track in an emergency, an audience appreciates being able to follow where you are in the presentation.

➡ Tip #4: Take strategic breaks to buy yourself a few minutes

Taking a strategic break is another technique a lost presenter can use. Have a prepared segue ready just in case a mental lapse occurs. "We've been covering some deep content for a while so let's just take a brief break." If you're really lost, have them stand (and not leave the room). This will take up a few more minutes and take the visual pressure off you. If you're in need of a briefer moment to collect your thoughts, keep them seated. The point is, make a break and do something less left brain to unplug the pressure and give the right brain a chance to help you. Returning then to the presentation gives you a chance to review notes, illustrations, etc, to find a place to jump in. Don't worry about being fluid at this point, just get the river flowing again. The audience is only looking for something, not everything, from your presentation.

➡ Tip #5: The fifteen-second mental recover plan

Prepare a routine for mental recovery in 10 or 15 seconds. It might go something like this:

1) Stop talking (no point babbling when you are lost)

2) Tighten and relax your fists and toes

3) Take two deep breaths, one to get out the lost air and one to bring in the found air

4) Have an "if I'm lost story" ready on an index card to help make your main point

5) Skip to the next point you know has not yet been covered.

The most important point is to have a practiced plan to reorient your presentation in case of blanking. Calming down, going to the next illustration, or using a story to bring you back, will help you to go on with the show.

The "two-minute drill" for presenters:
What to do when your presentation time is cut short

How many times have you been in the audience when you realize the sessions are running long, you're tired and hot, and the speaker is just beginning when the schedule indicates it's almost time to conclude? It may not be fun for you, but I guarantee you, it's no picnic for the presenter either. If you present very often, sooner or later you'll get crunched for time, and the need for your abbreviated presentation plan will become critical. Hopefully you'll have more than two minutes. Simply pushing through the content without regard to the clock is not an option.

➡ Tip #1: Tell your audience what they hope you already know

As you step to the podium, your audience is painfully aware of the fact things have run long. They've checked their watches and they are praying you've checked yours. Putting them at ease requires just a single well-rehearsed statement to your audience:

"I know it's late and I'll limit my thoughts today to just a few important ones that will be valuable to you."

It doesn't need to be more than that. You've acknowledged the challenge. Making apologies about all the good stuff they're going to miss only sets you up for lowered audience expectations. Your goal now is to make your comments rich and concise. Gone are the long stories or in-depth descriptions.

➡ Tip #2: Cue off your presentation summary slides

As described in the Presentation Planner document earlier in this guide, it's essential that every presenter have a strong sense of the three to four primary presentation messages. Those messages are covered in opening comments and agenda slides and are a critical element in your presentation close. The time remaining will determine the right approach for you.

➡ Tip #3: Break your abbreviated presentation into thirds

Opening third. Starting with your title slide, deliver your opening comments/stories that set the stage as described in Presentation Survival Skill # 2. The well-rehearsed opener includes your personal introduction and creates a compelling bridge to your main messages.

Middle third. Move quickly to your presentation summary slide. Those three to four main points will become talking points for the next few minutes. Create a one-minute summary of each of those main points. Skip the detail or you will exceed your time budget quickly.

Closing third. Time to review Survival Skill #2 for how to create a strong presentation closer. This is where you plan to "stick the landing" and have already rehearsed the summary closing statements augmented by a story or other personal connection pulling all the pieces together.

Plan for an abridged presentation with PowerPoint's Custom Shows

The next time you're in your PowerPoint 97/2000 software, take a look under the Slide Show menu. You'll discover a little used option called Custom Shows. Custom Show provides you with an opportunity to define a custom path through all your presentation slides. If you've had enough foresight to anticipate the shortened presentation, go through the Custom Shows menu and define an abbreviated subset of slides that omit several layers of detail. Doing this is considerably easier in the privacy of your own office than on the fly in front of a live audience.

Then, when you're presented with the need for the shortened presentation, simply jump into the Slide Show menu to start your presentation and select the shortened show version. The omitted slides will be jumped over automatically and your audience will wonder how you were able to adapt so quickly.

Survival Summaries
Managing Fear

Since fear is generally anticipation of the unknown that affects the body, you can battle it with cognitive and physiological approaches.

- **Hook up to friendly faces**

    Talk to some of your audience members before the presentation so you can hook up early with friendly, "known" faces.

- **Humorous imaginations**

    These imaginations can moderate your fearful expectations.

- **Peaceful image**

    Recreate a relaxing mental image from memory including sensory information.

- **Integrate more structure into your presentation approach**

    As confidence returns, give yourself permission to take some additional freedoms.

- **Muscle tone**

    Work, warm, or wear-out muscle tightness and discover that some of that fear will melt away. Better to sweat before the presentation than during.

- **Take a few deep breaths**

    Sending additional oxygen to the brain will help the fog.

Survival Summaries
When you go blank

Anticipate that you will go blank at some point and therefore need a plan to get you through to the next point. Practicing the plan for getting lost will add an extra level of confidence that even if the worst occurs, you're prepared.

- **Memory devices**

    Use memory devices, such as the house walk, to keep track of your presentation progress.

- **Orientation**

    Have a set of illustrations or graphic material to rely on for orientation.

- **Visual clues**

    Create visual clues within the presentation screens.

- **Strategic break**

    Use a break to momentarily divert attention and give you time to mentally regroup.

- **Practiced plan**

    Build a specific, practiced plan to relax and reconnect.

Survival Summaries
When your time is cut short

- **Tell your audience what they already know**

    Assure them of your brevity, but tell them that you have a few thoughts you'd like to share with them. Don't lower their expectations of the value you're about to bring to them. Here's an example of a fifteen minute summary presentation:

- **Opening third**

    Deliver your prepared opening statements/stories as you had prepared for the original presentation. This sets the context and relevance that are essential even in a shortened presentation.

- **Middle third**

    Jump to your presentation summary slide and do a one-minute summary of each of the points.

- **Closing third**

    Hopefully, you've created a strong closing statement as described in Survival Skill #2. This pulls together all the key themes and personally connects them to your audience.

- **Keep to your time commitments**

    Finish when you indicated you would. Your audience will respect you for respecting them.

Survival Skill 6

Manage Your Presentation Environment

You're in the middle of a big presentation and disaster strikes: the adjoining dish room in the hotel comes alive with activity or perhaps the seating arrangements leave some audience members going through physical gymnastics to see presenter and presentation screens. Learn the five key areas related to managing your presentation environment from the selection of presentation background treatments that compliment room lighting to leveraging the room layout for maximum impact. One thing is for sure, we can never control all the variables and must learn to become more adaptive presenters.

Use environment-compatible graphics
Template design starts with knowing your presenting environment.

Line of sight – point of focus
See your presentation through your audience's eyes.

Manage your presentation technology
Make technology your ally in successful presenting.

Manage room sound
Support you and your laptop sound.

Manage room lighting
Recognize the challenges that can sink your next presentation.

Skill #6 – Manage Your Presentation Environment

> *"Any activity becomes creative when the doer cares about doing it right, or doing it better."*
> *– John Updike*

A Closer Look...
Use environment-compatible graphics

One size may frequently fit all when it comes to socks, baseball caps and sunglasses; but this principle rarely applies when it comes to presentations.

One morning, I had an appointment set up with a prospective client. I made the mistake of using his electronic projector when I had one I could have easily brought to the meeting. In the consulting and design business, the images you project on the wall say a lot about your level of expertise and prowess with the software tools. As we got to the critical moment in the presentation when I switched on the projector, I knew instantly this was going to be a bad morning. The meeting room had cold florescent lighting directly above the screen and the electronic projector provided by the client could only put out 350 meager lumens of light intensity. The subtly crafted and elegant template design samples and graphic treatments turned to a dull mush on screen. Gone were the rich colors, subtle background airbrush effects and soft drop shadows. Realizing that my ability to close this deal hung in the balance, I spun my laptop around to show them what the images would look like in a different environment. Too late, game over.

Sometimes we only get a single opportunity to make that impression. The environment can become a friend or enemy so consider these important design rules.

- **Lighter, brighter presentation rooms** with a great deal of ambient light will be better served by presentations with lighter background treatments and darker or black text and base artwork elements. If this sounds reminiscent of the old

overhead projection days in fully lit rooms, it's the same principle. The lighter colors will not wash out to a greater degree on screen and the darker elements will survive the additional harsh lighting. This template approach can also work well when you might incur more variable lighting conditions with a single presentation.

- **Presentation rooms with good lighting control** will allow you to subdue the lighting in and around the screen without the need to darken the entire room. The rich colors of a projected image will all be visible along with all the elegance of elements airbrushed into the template backgrounds using paint software packages for creating those backdrops. Rear screen projection also offers similar advantages.

The best template backgrounds create impressions but the subtle images won't survive harsh lighting.

Skill #6 – Manage Your Presentation Environment

Line of sight – point of focus

- **You're ready for the room, but is the room ready for you?**

  Seating can be a critical element in creating a speaker-focused room environment. Project your image to fill the screen and then spend a few minutes walking around the seats. Is the line of sight impaired or are chairs placed too far to the edges to see your projected visuals? Now is the time to take care of this with the onsite staff. For those presenters who like to be more mobile, the ability to create a middle aisle and close the distance with your audience from time to time can be an effective technique. As you move into the aisle and close the gap, attention levels will rise and your message becomes much more personal, but don't go there too often.

- **Podium placement**

  To podium or not to podium – that is the question. Podiums are a blessing and a curse, so consider these issues. Podiums can anchor your speaking position, keep you from wondering and hide nervous feet and hands. That's the good news. The bad news is that whenever you put anything between yourself and your audience, you create relational distance. You are perceived as more formal, and the inevitable pages of notes in front of you often causes you to take your eyes off your audience.

If you use a podium, be sure to make sure it's placed to the left of your presentation screen. From the time we were very small we learned that information flows left to right – anchor left, read right. Reverse this order by a right stage placement of the podium and your audience will experience a level of discomfort that they may not be able to articulate. My advice – present without a podium whenever possible and work on your body mechanics to minimize distracting movements.

◆ Platform height

Having an elevated platform can often provide a greater degree of visibility to a larger room full of people. However, in smaller settings, elevated platforms and the increased distance they create can have the unintended effect of creating an awkward space which impairs your ability to connect with your audiences and involve them in your presentation. You become just a distant talking head, your facial features indistinct, making it near impossible to create strong personal impressions.

An even larger issue can become the creaks and squeaks that often go hand in hand with raised platforms. It's unavoidable unless you immobilize yourself. If you must use a platform, know where you can go without creating those noisy interruptions! A little well-placed masking tape might be a wise idea.

Skill #6 – Manage Your Presentation Environment

♦ **Create more personal connections through movement**

As you place yourself to the left of your presentation screen, you will discover that there will be varying degrees of forward/back depth available to you. Nervous presenters tend to hide out in the back of the presenter's area and at the plane of the screen. Delivery skills consultant Tom Mucciolo has defined this space as the Presenter's Triangle*.

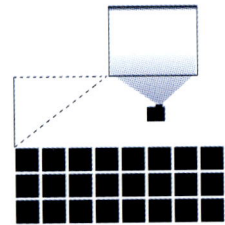

This space is created if you were to draw an imaginary line from the screen to the audience member most right of you and then back to the plane of the screen. Overly mobile presenters will move forward and out of that space. The key is in understanding how your position in the presenter's corner alters the focus and perceptions of an audience. As you move further back in the space and closer to the plane of the screen, the screen becomes the focal point. It's a lot bigger than you are and gains the attention momentarily. If your intent is to draw attention to screen graphics, stepping backward and toward the screen will refocus your audience's attention. Moving forward in the presenter's corner re-focuses attention on you once again. Moving to the extreme front of that space and at your closest point to the audience allows you to deliver personal stories or key points

*"*Purpose, Movement, Color*" by Tom Mucciolo
©1994

with added emphasis. Don't stay there too long, however, or you will desensitize your audience to that movement and that person space.

Manage your presentation technology

Any references to specific presentation technology would become quickly dated, but there are some universal concepts related to managing presentation technologies that apply to you today.

▶ **Laptop computers**

Today's laptop computers certainly have the horsepower to drive the typical business presentation, but here are some ideas for what's important in a laptop computer.

- Increase RAM to 128MB or better to minimize "lock-ups" by giving Windows more room to manage memory.

- Easily accessible sound controls will come in handy.

- If you will be using many mouse movements to click and select items, consider hooking up an external standard mouse avoiding the small laptop mouse.

- Know resolution terminology and implications:

VGA	640x480	Expect jaggy artwork and text.
SVGA	800x600	Good general detail & text clarity.
XGA	1024x768	Great detail for spreadsheets, screen captures and software demos.
SXGA	1280x1024	Extremely high level of detail with plenty of desktop real estate to lay out screens for demos.

▸ Utilizing a laptop's video out (NTSC) port

Many laptop computers on the market today now include a video out port which, in essence, converts your RGB computer signal to an NTSC signal. The idea is if you should only have access to a video monitor and not an electronic projector, you can still display your presentation. Bottom line, I would search high and low for an electronic projector of reasonable resolution before resorting to this approach. The significantly lower video resolution will negatively impact your presentation in several ways.

First, any smaller detail in your presentations like thin line widths and smaller fonts, will be noticeably degraded in quality. The thinner lines might even disappear from your external video monitor. Secondly, the color values that you observed on your computers monitor can change significantly. More saturated color values can become overly bold and obnoxious or even appear to pulsate a bit on screen. Overall, this should only be a final resort for presenters and if you're only faced with this option, give yourself time to view the converted presentation on the video monitor and make appropriate changes.

▸ More on portable electronic projectors

Because of the expense of the early electronic projectors, many companies are still hanging on to them for dear life. Here are some things to know about your electronic projector:

350-500 lumens	Adequate in very dark smaller rooms
500-750 lumens	Good in darker small to medium size rooms
750-1000 lumens	Excellent in most small to medium room scenarios with controlled lighting.
1500+ lumens	Strong image in larger room environments accomodating several hundred with greater ambient lighting.

▸ Connectivity issues

The connection of computer to electronic projector can still be an inexact science. Follow these important guidelines:

- Try to marry laptop and projector of the same resolution so changes in the laptops native resolution are not required.

- Tighten down all connections. Loose connections can cause unplanned loss of signal or strange color shifts.

- During set-up, turn on the laptop first, then the projector so the projection system will have an image to "lock on" to during boot-up.

- Newer digital projectors will make connectivity to laptops that can produce a digital signal a snap - instant lock and load of signal.

- A PC laptop computer typically utilizes an Fn (function key) to create 3 laptop display views; laptop display only, external monitor only or both. These three states are achieved through toggling through the options by holding down your Fn function key and then selecting the F8 or equivalent key on your laptop that controls display viewing.

Skill #6 – Manage Your Presentation Environment

- Set the laptop & screen refresh rate through the display menu to 60 Hz. for better connectivity.

Manage room sound

Balancing sound in a hotel meeting room will take some trial and error. An unnaturally amplified voice will take what could have been a personal presentation and give it a large impersonal auditorium flavor. Balance the volume to create a comfortable listening environment.

➡ Tip #1 Use a cordless microphone

Use a cordless lapel mike whenever possible to give you the freedom of movement without having to worry about a restricting umbilical cord or podium microphone. Feeling tethered like a puppy is one preoccupation that you don't need. Fresh batteries, however, are a must. Be sure to have some handy.

➡ Tip 2: Increasing your presentation sound support

Once you've established a good volume level, consider how you will be supporting the sound elements that might be coming from your laptop computer. Whether they're voice-overs, music or appropriate sound effects, they will not carry adequately from the small laptop speakers. Always bring along the extra patch-type cords that may be required to get from your laptop (typically "mini-stereo" plugs) to 1/4" male jacks and mini-stereo to two "phono" plugs. Many times, hotels will not have those adaptors readily available, causing you to run up to the last seconds awaiting the presentation before someone shows up with the right plugs (if at all). Although the house or room sound systems can adequately handle the sound, you might want to run the sound into your electronic projector and test its adequacy to support the room size. If the room size is too large, then run through the "audio out" jack on many projectors to the house system. By doing this, your projector provides localized sound-fill while the house covers the rest, creating a well-balanced orchestration of sound. You also need a sound cable long enough to run to the house sound. Ideally, you will have an easily-accessible volume control on your laptop during the presentation to act as a master sound control.

Manage room lighting

In many hotel or conference settings, each room has a number of different room setup configurations based on the specific needs of the group.

➡ Tip #1 Know where to control lighting

Check out where your lighting controls are located. Dimmer switches are ideal because you can dim the ambient light to the point that it makes your colors crisp and bright on screen but not so dark that your audience is tempted to catnap to get caught up on their jet lag.

➡ Tip #2 Determine best mix for you and your presentation

Determine your control points. Make sure you are able to control the lighting directly above the actual screen. Remember, where your screen is located now was where a buffet table was a few hours earlier. Don't count on hotels to understand the nuances of your personal presentation set up. Make sure that your electronic projector can be placed at a reasonable distance from the screen to create the image size necessary for the group.

Excessive or uncontrolled lighting can make your presentation colors blah and lifeless; with more control of your lighting options, colors can come alive.

Shrink Wrap
Dr. Scott Lee
Environmental Overload

I must admit that I love the look of a long, straight drive in golf. Tiger Woods' play appeals to me because he hits so consistently straight and long. For a shrink I'm not a half bad golfer. My drives are long and my irons always seem to find the target from 175 yards out. Then there's my wedge, probably my favorite club which can put the ball consistently up near the pin.

But then – when I leave the driving range – life seems to take a nasty turn. **Something happens to me when the shots actually count on the scorecard and there are trees and water hazards everywhere**. My long and straight shots degrade into tree-seeking missiles and my irons become the equivalent of a graphite-shafted Ditch Witch. You don't even want to know about my wedge.

What happened? And why does this seem to happen to so many of us? I believe the answer lies in two little words: anxiety and focus. When there is no risk to my shots, my body relaxes and my swing is simply smoother and more instinctual. When I'm on the course and it's for real those things around me like trees, ponds and the stares of those in my foursome steal my focus. The harder I try to stay away from trouble, the more trouble seems to seek me out. Dangerous game this golf. My focus becomes the potential trouble – not a relaxed, comfortable swing.

A similar process takes place when we present to an audience. We quickly become aware of the potential danger all around us and we overcompensate by holding back and playing into the middle of the "fairway." Safe and short may not be a bad idea on the golf course but this approach in a presentation is a sure recipe for mediocrity.

You're mentally prepared for a one-on-one with your manager and her boss decides to sit in as well. The room lighting makes your presentation look like pea soup or you discover you're one plug-in short in the meeting room – all these "surprises" can quickly take us out of our game. **When we experience anxiety, we often play our presentation more close to the vest**. Maybe we don't tell that personal story we practiced because we're now not sure we can tell it well. Our body tenses up, our speech becomes halting or pressured, we forget the well-honed transition statements and our presentation becomes choppy compared to our practice runs.

The main point here is one you've heard before: the most significant part of any presentation is the presenter. Focus precedes success.

Be aware that the environment in which you're presenting is dynamic, it is constantly changing. What does not change is your role. You are the one who brings the new idea, plan or concept. It's time to rest in the fact that you are there and not someone else because you have something unique to contribute. The more focused your audience becomes on you, the less aware they will be of their environment. Here are some ideas:

- Get there early to acclimate to the presentation environment.
- Know your presentation inside and out.
- Program your mind with a well-delivered outcome just like your golf shot. The body will respond with a smooth presentation if the mind says it's ok. Take a few risks.
- Be confident in your message. Don't pull back on the stories; have some fun.
- Trust your instincts and not your fears

You've now separated yourself from the ranks of the merely average.

Survival Summaries

- **Template design considerations**
  - High ambient light or low lumen projectors.

    Use lighter backgrounds, dark text, accents and graphics.

  - Controlled room lighting or high lumen projector:

    Use darker, richer backgrounds, light text, accents and graphics.

- **Room set-up**

  Before the event, pick four very different seats to sit in and gain an audience perspective on hearing, seeing and participating in your presentation. If more audience interaction is necessary, seats should be arranged so that the participants can see each other, as well as the presenter (i.e., in a half-circle). If chairs are placed into smaller groupings, keep them in groups no more than ten with an ideal of eight to a group.

- **Technology set-up**

    Your projector and laptop become the most essential technology elements in any presentation. Use the same resolution for the laptop and projector when possible. Switching laptop resolutions is not always ideal and takes some trial and error. Turn the laptop computer on first, then the projector. Remember the best technology is invisible technology.

- **Sound set-up**

    If you're plugging in a laptop to house sound, travel with extra adaptors: mini stereo 1/8" to 1/4", BNC and phono. Use a cordless lapel when possible to give you untethered freedom of movement and control your laptop sound via the laptop sound controls and not house system adjustments.

- **Lighting set-up**

    Learn the degree of lighting control that exists. Some house systems have a number of presets you can leverage. Lights over projection screens wash out color and contrast. Too dark, you lose eye contact. Find just the right balance.

- **Be an adaptive presenter**

    Learn to overcome your environment with a strong grasp of message and delivery.

Survival Skill 7

Hone the Art of Presenting

Let's face it, there simply aren't enough hours in the day to try to get good at everything we need to do. There are certain things I've resigned myself to where I will never be great. Good maybe, average at worst, but not great. The art of presenting is a unique activity in our lives because it transcends the personal and the professional. Your ability to craft and deliver a solid presentation message may take the form of a college thesis, job interview or strategic partner meeting. Whatever it may look like for you, presenting has never been more critical to your personal success. Survival Skill #7 offers some practical ideas on how you can fine tune your presentation approaches and still keep your day job.

The important role of coaches and mentors
We can't become good presenters without some help.

Get up to bat as often as you can!
Infrequent presenters are rarely good presenters.

Get your creativity out-of-the-box
Finding creative inspiration

Hire a presentation professional
Getting your presentation up to speed quickly.

Exceed your "personal best" efforts
A healthy approach for gauging personal improvement.

Skill #7 – Hone the Art of Presenting

> *"Don't be afraid to give up the good for the great."*
> *– Kenny Rogers*

A Closer Look...
The important role of coaches and mentors

Being a golf hack, I was glued to my television set in July '99 watching the British Open golf tournament. I have to admit, it was kind of fun watching even the pros badly slice a drive into the visitor's gallery. But what really caught my attention was the role that the caddy played with these pro golfers. Lest you think they're just lackeys who carry the clubs from hole to hole, watch a little closer - especially on the putting greens. What you'll see is a very different relationship than what you might first expect. There's a real partnership with the caddy. He plays a very proactive role in which club to use, where he thinks a putting green might break or how to play a difficult shot out of the rough.

As the golf drama played out, one golfer had a commanding lead going into the last hole and only had to play mediocre golf to win the match. Instead of playing it safe, the pro grabbed his driver and proceeded to the tee. The caddy failed to challenge a very poor club selection, which ultimately led to the golfer losing the competition. You think the caddy's role is insignificant? It cost the pro (and the caddy) a huge payday and the honor that went along with winning the prestigious British Open.

We're a society that takes pride in our independence.

When it comes to your presentation skills, however, you become the worst evaluator of your own performance.

You're too close and your lack of objectivity perspective means you can fool yourself about your real effectiveness. Partner with another presenter/coach and commit to being at one another's presentations as often as possible. Here are the keys to a successful partnership and how to best assess your improvements:

- If possible, partner with a peer, not a boss.
- Have a mutual commitment to each other's personal development.
- Be honest and provide balanced feedback. Praise the good, articulate the areas for improvement.
- Provide consistent feedback by making an evaluation checklist that you use every time. Here are some examples of relevant elements of assessment:

Vocal mechanics

When you get nervous, do you tend to talk faster? Is your speech often laced with distracting "umms" and "ahhhs"? You're unaware of those until you hear yourself on tape. Video recording a presentation or two can be a real eye opener. Those with more of a monotone delivery may find that audiences will struggle to stay engaged after 20 minutes or so. Varying the highs and lows and creating more vocal variety can often help. Also, the ability to articulate your words so they're clear and crisp will make your voice easier to listen to, keeping the audience engaged longer.

Presentation content

Does it flow well or does it get bogged down in non-essential areas? Does key messaging stand out in the presentation or is it a blur of themes? Have stories been used to personalize content to the audience? How relevant did you make the information?

Presentation graphics

Does the quality of the graphics fit the venue? (Professionally crafted images for professional audiences?) Are charts clear and easy to understand? Does each presentation screen reflect the adherence to the seven-second rule? (See Survival Skill #4)

Presentation delivery

Were hand gestures and movements smooth or distracting? Does there seem to be reoccurring presenting habits that need to be addressed? Do you use the space well to create different levels of emphasis and personalization?

Use of technology

Many presenters wear their presentation technology like a badge of honor. The state-of-the-art laptop, high-resolution projector and remote point device are proudly displayed like a shiny new sports car. To extend this little metaphor, remember you're the sports car. Your technology is simply the unseen engine under the hood. It empowers but never upstages. It equips but is always a silent partner. Do you leverage the technology behind your presentation seamlessly? Are your screen images advanced or animations built without undo fanfare? Do you find yourself constantly apologizing for distracting technology issues?

Getting "up to bat" often

Maybe you're not into baseball, but let's see if I can prompt you to think of a few famous baseball players from recent history: Ken Griffey Jr., Mark McGwire, Sammy Sosa. During the season, these players are honing their skills in games three or four times a week and when they're not playing, they're working with coaches on specific skills. How good do you think Mark McGwire would be if he only got up to bat once a month? Once every two months? The answer is, not very good.

As a presenter, it's pretty tough to hone your skills when you present infrequently.

When too much time has elapsed between outings, it's difficult to fine-tune your skills. Here are some ways to increase your opportunities. If you are fearful of presenting, the idea of going out and looking for places to present may seem like dodging cars on the freeway, but nonetheless, it is important to you and your chosen career, so here goes:

- To help build some confidence, take the initiative to do internal company presentations to friendly audiences.

- Tradeshows often need speakers to support specific topic areas. They're usually 60 minute or less opportunities and perfect for polishing your skills.

- During sales calls, co-present with another presenter and attempt to deliver that same segment several times a week.

Time to get your creativity out of the box!

If getting creative with the design and graphics of your presentation is a challenge, you're not alone. For most presenters, the sole source of their inspiration is other presenters. This explains why so few presentations ever rise above the average. The key to expanding your list of possibilities is looking beyond the world of business presentations to other mediums that have created interesting visual imagery to make their point. Here are just a few ideas:

- **Charts**. Check out the charts that are being created in the USA Today, Newsweek, the six o'clock news or other progressive media sources.

  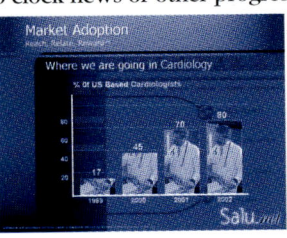

  You can bet they're not using stock treatments; but the big surprise is, they're not more complicated, just more clever. This means you might be creating more charts manually, but it's the only way to get beyond the bland look that stock charting templates provide.

- **Illustrations.** Often we see overly detailed spreadsheets, scanned letters or advertisements where the actual information is totally illegible.

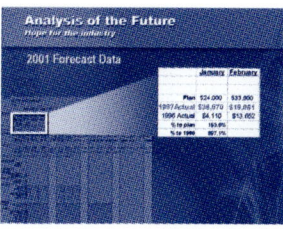

Why business presenters continue to import and use those images may be a testament to how easy it is to import graphics but not to good common sense. Watch the TV program 60-Minutes and see how they blow out lines of text from complicated letters or documents. They don't expect you to read the small print. They provide the graphic as a point of reference and then draw your attention through "blown-out" detail to the real meat of the message. Similar effects can be created in PowerPoint.

- **Benchmarks for artwork quality.** If you want to know what's appropriate for the quality of graphics in your presentations, grab a few nicely done brochures or company annual reports. After all, they're just other business communication tools and the same level of graphic appropriateness should apply. Here's a list of the items you <u>won't</u> find:
    - "Cute" clipart
    - Lines that don't line up correctly
    - Images that inappropriately overlap
    - Poor quality scanned photos
    - Bad logos grabbed from the Internet
    - Badly combined color choices
    - Misaligned artwork

Skill #7 – Hone the Art of Presenting

Hire a presentation professional and learn the tricks

Why would you consider hiring a design professional to do your first business presentation? After all, PowerPoint is sitting right there on your desktop. Any bonehead can create a few quick slides. I have a question for you. Microsoft Publisher might be there too, so why aren't you creating your own brochures? FrontPage is front and center but I'm guessing you're not creating the company website either. Let's try one more. Microsoft Access is there, but you're probably not creating database front-ends here.

There are times when it's easy to identify the stakes associated with the results generated from a professionally-crafted business presentation. Go to school on the presentation design professionals. Learn what they know and, because you have the application as well, dissect their efforts and see how they leveraged the tools and design elements. Here are a few ideas to consider before hiring a professional:

- **Check out their portfolio** in the presentation software you are currently using. Do they significantly raise the bar in the skills they bring?

- Talk to their customers about the caliber of the presentation graphics as well as the quality of the **process of creating and approving presentation elements.**

- If developing the actual message is a challenge, partner with a company that can help you create the graphics and also work directly with you on

how to create an appropriate presentation message from your current presentation content.

- **Negotiate the rights** to the native graphics and template artwork (in PhotoShop, PhotoPaint, etc.) up front if you plan to start working directly with those elements in the future. They aren't necessarily included with the project pricing.
- Take an active role in the process and **ask questions** about how (and why) they created certain artwork.

It has little to do with the software you use

Putting together a presentation that's a creative work of art is not always as easy as you're led to believe. With all the freedom your presentation software provides today (16.8 million color choices, hundreds of obscure chart types and auto shapes that won't quit), most business presenters today manage to create some pretty benign looking presentations.

Lest you think that spending a few extra dollars on a presentation software package is always the key to more dazzling multimedia presentations, think again.

Yea, the effects are all there, but there's more to making good presentation than a set of software features as long as your arm. It's way too easy to create some pretty ugly furniture with some expensive woodworking tools. On the flip side, it's also very difficult to create attractive wood projects with only a basic complement of tools. As in woodworking, crafting a professional looking presentation takes either a balance of tools and talent or the budget to hire someone who does.

Next time you're putting together your presentation and there's a lot on the line, consider these tools for maximizing the impact of your next presentation.

The delivery vehicle

At its most fundamental level, your presentation software package is simply the means to orchestrate and deliver text and images that tell a compelling business message. It's a delivery mechanism. The biggest challenge you'll have in creating professional and visually-rich presentation content is when you believe that your favorite presentation software encapsulates all the elements you need to create powerful presentations. Granted, there are a lot of components available like clipart, stock templates and drawing tools to choose from but presentations that hope to rise above the sea of mediocrity will need to leverage software tools better suited for some of the more custom design task requirements. The true "power" in PowerPoint-type applications is ultimately how easy it is to integrate and orchestrate external elements that make PowerPoint look anything but "just a PowerPoint presentation." After all, when's the last time you flipped through an in-flight magazine and admired the Adobe Illustrator advertisements?

Case Study

I received a call from a Canadian customer who was interested in Distinction evaluating the caliber of their sales presentation. They were using Astound because they wanted the advanced multimedia and design features that the software promised. In discussions that followed, it became clear there were additional dynamics for their choice of software. The slightly longer learning curve associated with that product made it possible for several members of their staff to become "experts," while creating a certain level of job security. Very few people could control the development process. At this point, I was curious about their presentation so I asked them to forward it on.

What I received taught me an important lesson about the presentation design process. There was nothing in the presentation, short of a few transition effects, that couldn't have been done in PowerPoint. The sales messages weren't very crisp. The graphics were standard fare with a few new pieces of basic clipart. The bulleted text was much too long.

Bottom line, the extra cost for the software bought them nothing. Truly good presentations are made up of many important elements, the least of which are all the special goodies and features you find in presentation software today.

Presentation software can make the job easier, but it can't guarantee good presentations. That's totally up to you.

Exceeding your "personal best" benchmarks

Last summer, I helped put together a golf tournament for a dozen or so of my buddies. I usually don't lower myself to trash-talking the opposition, but they were clearly superior golfers and I had to get inside their heads well in advance of the event. The only problem was that sooner or later, I had to actually come through with a decent round of golf. I

Skill #7 – Hone the Art of Presenting

even got so desperate that the week before I spent an hour with a local golf pro and learned seven things to think about when I swing my golf club. After an hour on the driving range, I realized that instead of slicing with the grace of an instinctual swing, I now was duck hooking (even worse) because I was concentrating so hard on doing all seven things just right! (Now I will gladly pay for a few lessons for my most challenging opponents.)

Unless you're the rare individual, one or two things to work on for improvement in any specific presentation are more than enough.

Despite the temptation to compare yourself with those presenters around you, don't do it. In most cases you will be setting your sights too low. Track and field athletes have the right idea. They're constantly working on improving their last best personal effort. Learn from others, but push yourself to improve your own standards. Here are some ways you can exceed your personal best efforts on your next presentation.

- **Intentionally choose to only work on two new things.** During your next presentation sort through the input provided you by others and identify one or two things to improve in your next presentation (i.e., keep your hands at your sides, keep your bullets more succinct, break down that complex chart that has glazed your audience's eyes for months…).

- **Don't lose ground from your last presentation effort.** Continuous improvement can be a way of life. Build your skill base each time you present!

- **Don't be diverted from your goals.** Don't defocus your efforts by becoming preoccupied with presenters who are significantly better or worse than you are. Learn but don't mimic.

Shrink Wrap
Dr. Scott Lee
If at first you don't succeed…

How come some presentations go smoothly and others are an uphill battle? Perhaps one of the reasons may come from a psychological term called the Premack Principle.

I used to sing in a gospel quartet that wasn't too bad. Our rehearsals focused on learning, memorizing, and performing various songs. It was usually late at night, after several attempts at a better sound, when one of the members would say the equivalent of "enough already. Let's go home." But I have learned in my graduate studies and in performing that **the way you last practiced your presentation is most likely the way you will present it next.** We would stay and get it right, then go home.

This is called the Premack Principle. It has to do with a certain type of brain encoding which believes that your practice may be your reality. Your brain remembers your experience and does its own rehearsal unconsciously. If you make a big mistake in practice and do not correct it, the brain continues to rehearse the mistake and your next performance is likely to include it. So, it is not enough to practice your presentation over and over, it is critical to practice doing it correctly to enhance the likelihood of a smooth presentation the next time.

Survival Summaries

- **Find a good peer coach/mentor**

    Partner with someone who can provide an objective assessment of your content, graphics and delivery on a regular basis. Be honest and balanced in your feedback.

- **Get up to bat frequently**

    Infrequent presenters rarely improve. Take every opportunity to deliver presentations. Frequent presenters are learning presenters.

- **Presentation content**

    Look for ideas for presentation content in unusual places like the six o'clock news, brochures, US Today or magazine charts. They're frequently simple but tell a story all by themselves and often avoid the charting pitfalls exhibited by the casual presenter.

- **Focus on a just a few things to improve in your next presentation**

    Don't try to do a dozen things differently. Choose one or two specific areas to exceed your previous "personal best" efforts. Experiment, explore, celebrate your victories and learn from your mistakes.

- **Presentation design professional**

    Get up to speed more quickly by hiring a presentation design professional. A truly unique business communication medium requires unique approaches to content, graphics and delivery. Hire a professional presentation designer the first time around and notice how s/he designs backgrounds, lay out graphics, treats text and tastefully animates key messages.

Survival Skill 8

Create and Deliver Internet-based Presentations

How tough could it be? After all, your presentation software said all you had to do was "Save as HTML" and your laptop presentation could easily be re-purposed for web presenting – or can it? Years ago those who had a talent for desktop publishing saw the Internet as a nice little design area to add to their resume. They quickly learned differently. They discovered that the Internet demanded an entirely different set of design requirements and software tools. In the same way, the Internet introduces a number of new considerations for presentation design. Survival Skill #8 will help prepare you for delivering your next web presentation.

Options for web-based presentations
Know your online options.

Designing good Internet presentation templates
A good web presentation starts with an appropriate template.

Unique content development requirements
Web design issues the presenter needs to consider.

Delivering Internet presentations
Preparing to deliver a presentation to an unseen audience.

Skill #8 – Create and Deliver Internet-based Presentations

A Closer Look...
Options for web-based presentations

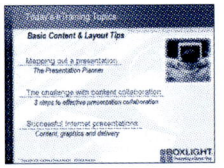

There are a number of ways to leverage presentations on the web. The method you choose will be determined by your goals for that presentation and the experience you want the visitor to have. Here are some options for your consideration:

Post it for download

Often, it's not critical for the web visitor to physically view each frame of the presentation via their browser. It's more important to be able to get the presentation back to the desktop/laptop for use or viewing later. For example, if you missed a conference speaker and their presentation was made available, place a thumbnail view of the title slide along with a description, file size, and the link that allows the visitor to simply click and download the presentation back to their computer from your website.

➡ **PRO's:** You don't need to recreate the template and graphics for 8-bit web viewing. Presentation animations don't need to be eliminated and screens rebuilt for manual build slides.

➡ **CON's:** Time to download on a slower Internet connection. There's always the possibility the viewer does not have the presentation software you used or has an older, unsupported version.

Convert it to HTML

If you've considered all the implications (covered later in this section) of converting your presentation to HTML, save out those files and have your webmaster post those for viewing. Most presentation software applications will give the user some traditional button navigation options to move through the presentation slides.

➡ **PRO's:** Your existing laptop presentation can be leveraged without recreating new HTML content for each screen.

➡ **CON's:** Potential serious compromise of colors when optimized back to 8-bit images. A significant amount of individual files are created and require management. In most cases, animations/transitions need to be stripped from the presentation. What you see is not always what you get.

Web-conferencing services

Today, e-conferencing companies have sprung up that have made a business out of providing hosting services for an online virtual meeting. These services generally include the sending of invitations (electronic and direct mail),

Skill #8 – Create and Deliver Internet-based Presentations

registration, training, coordination and a presentation assistant to help track real-time audience questions. All the technical details become their problem. Augmented only by your voice over a phone (or streamed via Real Audio over the web), you become the audible host for the presentation that you lead and navigate. Attendees follow along and are provided with opportunities to ask questions and respond electronically, creating instant feedback to the presenter. The presentation experience can be made even richer by pulling up a web site, static images, annotating key points or in higher-speed access scenarios, view video, animation or even you. When dealing with a more diverse broad-based audience, however, most e-conferencing companies don't attempt to stream audio or video over the Internet. It's just too risky and degrades the experience for low bandwidth attendees. For more information check out **www.placeware.com**, **www.evoke.com** or **www.webex.com**.

➡ *PRO's:* They take on all the technical concerns you might have with start-to-finish coordination of all the variables. The registration issues can all be coordinated for you. Some smaller web-conferencing venues for fewer participants are free. Database support can track audience participation level and attendance patterns.

➡ *CON's:* There is a cost associated with their support. Get it documented up front. Don't expect them to provide creative assistance. They're typically administration and IT professionals, not content or design experts.

Designing good Internet presentation templates

When designing presentation content, one of the first questions I ask a client is, "where will the presentation be used?" It makes all the difference in how it will look. I received a call from one such client who was concerned with the appearance of their template some three months after we designed it. It didn't take long to discover that in an effort to "leverage" their template investment, they were now using the presentation on their web site and it didn't even look close to the appearance on their laptop computers. "Save as HTML" is not a single simple solution for designing a web presentation template. Here are some essential considerations:

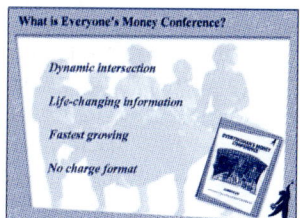

If 70-80% of what an audience retains is what they see, this venue for presenting places significantly more weight on the quality of the images displayed. Without the benefit of eye contact and body language, your screen images are the sole visual stimulus to keep your audience engaged. To complicate the issue, presentations on the web will generally need to be "dumbed down" graphically to accommodate a broad range of attendee viewing requirements and much shorter web attention spans.

Design for the lowest bandwidth visitor

Unless you have an extremely captive, high bandwidth audience, you must consider how quickly the graphical images will load from your web server to the visitor's desktop. Since the template graphics make up the bulk of the graphical load a user experiences, consider these basic custom web template guidelines:

Use spot color

Consider starting with a white background and use elements of corporate color to accent the template. In PowerPoint, that would mean using your drawing tools to create tasteful spot color edge treatments while adding in a clean, appropriately-colored logo.

Keep template text larger than normal

Some logos may have tag lines that are a part of every template. Just remember that many might be viewing your presentation at a lower resolution and the text that was readable at 1024x768 resolution is illegible at 800x600.

Custom designing a bitmap background for web presentations

Some presentation designers like to transcend the world of hard edge vector-based graphics to more elegant bitmap images created in paint programs like Adobe PhotoShop. If you were creating templates for your laptop computer, you would stay at 24-bit color display since your laptop can render all those colors in bright detail. For web presentations, however, you reduce the number of working colors to 8-bit (256 colors) because there can be a great deal of color compromise if files are later forced to 8-bit via presentation software or service bureau conversaion. Simply put, the smooth gradients (at 24-bit) become more blocky and pixilated at 8-bit. Soft drop shadows created on logos become less smooth and more solid in appearance.

Use a template already created for web use

Most presentation software applications will provide you with templates that should work well on the web. Be discerning, however. Some are better than others so don't let the graphics take precedent over the message. The more colors and full color treatments, the more time it will take for the screen to refresh on a visitor's screen who's viewing the page via a dial-up modem.

Unique content development requirements

Approach to content

Some web presentations are hosted –**synchronous** (delivered by someone while viewed via web browser), while others allow you

to view whenever you want –**asynchronous**. In either case, you have some unique challenges associated with this web medium. Since there is no physical presenter to provide body language or other visual clues, the total visible impact of your presentation will be based on the images you choose to illustrate and how quickly you move through them. It becomes even more essential to augment text messages with some sort of graphical reinforcement. The graphics need to be large and clean. The flow of content needs to be increased in pace significantly for delivered web presentations, moving between screens at a faster pace.

Basic artwork

Keep your presentation text larger and basic. In web presentations, it's even more critical to manage text because web attention spans have an even lower tolerance for reading without other stimulus. Add to that the fact that some visitors may have lower resolution monitors and it becomes a compelling reason to keep text simple and neat.

Use spot artwork to constantly reinforce messages. Just like clipart in a laptop presentation can create an overly informal and unprofessional appearance, choose your presentation support artwork carefully. Logos don't need to look bad on the web, but need to be created and viewed for their quality and appearance.

Presentation animations

In an effort to engage your audience, your laptop-based presentation may have included everything from animated text bullets to bar charts with bars animated on a mouse-click. The Internet and web browsers play by a different set of viewing rules, however. No matter what type of web presentation you deliver, it will only support your animations in a specific set of assumptions (For example, PowerPoint 2000 presentations saved to HTML and viewed with Internet Explorer 5.0). Since few presenters can define their visitors so finitely, you will need to strip all movement from your presentations. No transitions. No animations. Drop shadows make go away. Even when introducing text information that's built on screen, it will need to be created one slide at a time. Perhaps future browser versions can standardize on supporting rules for animations, but for now it's not the case.

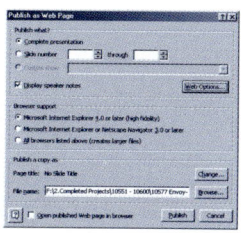 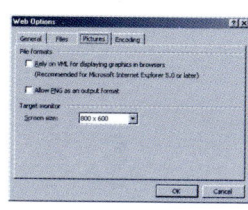

Presentation sound

Those sound effects that are so easily embedded into your presentations can be lost in the HTML environment. Once again, only in the most defined of situations will your small sound file download to the viewer's desktop and play. Sound is downloaded behind the scenes and played when ready. The audio is "streamed" to the desktop with the support of a player utility which the visitor will need to have to experience the audio.

Delivering Internet presentations

At some point in the future, you may be leading a web presentation. As the bandwidth issues are gradually resolved and the majority of visitors are

Skill #8 – Create and Deliver Internet-based Presentations

unimpaired by dial-up modem speeds, web presenting will become more commonplace. Perhaps you'll even be delivering video-conferences, but for now, there are some issues to consider the next time you find yourself leading a web presentation.

Pacing

You'll need to move quickly between screens. All they have to support the presentation are your carefully crafted screens and a disembodied voice. For that reason, target a 30-second to one minute maximum per screen. Our natural inclination to rush when we get nervous needs to be overcome. Create a comfortable and natural pace.

Voice inflection

Without your cheery smile, hand gestures and embracing body language, all they have of you is your voice. All the very best speaking skills you learned as a traditional presenter will need to be accentuated in this environment. Passion, excitement, appropriate pauses, and using your entire vocal range need to be exercised. I see a whole new class of presentation consultants in the future who assist presenters with managing their vocal delivery.

"Checking in"

Because your presentation visitors will be sitting at the comfort of their own desktops, they will be tempted to fall back into old multitasking habits when their attention lapses or an interesting email hits their desktop. For that reason, you will need to intrude into their activity every seven to eight minutes. If you're using web conferencing services, you can place "polling questions," or the equivalent, that causes your audience to periodically respond to your questions. If you have a smaller audience, pose a question on screen and solicit verbal responses from the group.

Duration

Web presentations need to be shorter than traditional presentations - period. If you planned a 60-minute presentation in person, a 30-minute version for web viewing is very appropriate. You simply will not be able to cover the information in the same level of detail. Can't crunch it down? Plan a morning session and an afternoon session of shorter duration.

Also, when delivering your presentation to a number of people in a remote location, have your presentation electronically projected on screen in a conference room where all the attendees are viewing together. Place your voice on a centrally located speakerphone, and the influence of the group dynamics will allow you to conduct longer Internet presentations.

Set expectations for level of detail

Because of the nature of the presentation venue, it becomes impossible to go into very much detail unless the entire session is dedicated to a single, specific topic. Even then, it's important to set audience expectations for the level of detail they're about to receive. It's a unique venue and, for the foreseeable future, will limit how you approach content compared to traditional face-to-face alternatives.

"Experience is a hard teacher. She gives the test first and the lessons afterwards."
– Anonymous

Shrink Wrap
Dr. Scott Lee
Being virtually personal

I used to live in the Greenwood area of Seattle, just across the street from Ken's Market. There are a lot of advantages to living across the street from the neighborhood market - you could actually run across the street and pick up some parmesan cheese and butter for the popcorn during a commercial break on Monday Night Football! But perhaps the most significant advantage was that you would see your neighbors and get to know the workers at the market.

Seeing your neighbors, knowing who is around you, and having predictable surroundings lead to a comfortable, more secure living environment and greater trust of others.

With the growth of business and industry within the city and the move of residences into suburban developments, there are fewer and fewer Ken's Markets. Rather, we shop at shopping centers miles from home where we do not see our neighbors. We commute long distances to work in a preferred setting. We drive across town to attend church or synagogue, we go to the swimming pool at the best facility and have our kids attend out of area schools to better their educational experiences. We have become a disconnected society wherein we do not know most of our neighbors, and not many others know us either. Remember what the "Cheers" television show used to say? Its great to have a place "where everybody knows your name."

Enter the Internet. It's a fantastic tool for connecting business, interest groups, and individuals. The only problem is that it is even more impersonal than our depersonalized society. We can enter chat rooms where we build friendships with others we have never seen and without any common experience. We attend conferences where we do not see the speaker, and we network with others without awareness of their facial expressions, body language, etc. **Depersonalization lends itself to lack of attention, lack of belief, and lack of trust.** Our world grows smaller and smaller because we cannot get the human details we need to extend ourselves relationally with others.

It is imperative as Internet presenters that we seek to make personal connections with our audience to minimize the experience of depersonalization. Using names from the registration list during your talk, or sharing common experiences with your audience (such as referring to the great baseball "subway series of 2000" when talking to a New York audience) or referencing recent national events such as the presidential debates or elections allows you to find common ground with the audience. Artwork that reveals humor, like relevant cartoons, or shared common experience makes a human connection. Sharing personal stories further allows the audience to paint a human picture of you, as well as taking time to describe your surroundings or even attire as you present (if you're still in your boxers or presenting from your bathtub, you might skip this last suggestion…).

Making human connections with your Internet audience is possible, and it is necessary. We are a fast-paced, always on the go society, but we continue to value real humans around us. Take your best shot, as a human, with your Internet audience and they will find your presentations more enjoyable, believable, and persuasive.

Survival Summaries

➡ **Understand your goals**

Consider all your options for web presenting.

➡ **Unique approaches**

Web presentations require unique approaches to content, flow and design compared to traditional laptop presenting.

➡ **Enhanced emphasis**

Web presentation delivery creates enhanced emphasis on voice inflection, pacing and interaction.

Survival Skill 9

Survive Q&A Sessions

Maybe you've always considered the Q and A session at the end of your presentation a necessary evil. After all, why would anyone subject themselves to the random questions of an exit-restless crowd? And why would you ever want to get off your prepared text into interactive no-mans land? The answer is that your question and answer times are simply an extension of your presentation and a final opportunity to drive your key theme through audience interaction. It's not a last minute add-on nor a time filler. It's an important time to embrace audience questions as the last presentation chapter. Now that we're in (near) agreement on that, here's how to get the most out of audience questions and answers and how to avoid some question and answer pitfalls.

The "co-presenter"

"I have things to say that everyone will want to hear"

Stump the presenter

"I'm smarter than you are"

Men are from Mars, women, boys, cats, dogs...

Off topic, off the planet

"Excuse me, I wasn't listening"

"Would you kindly repeat your presentation?"

124 | Skill #9 – Survive Q&A Sessions

Shrink Wrap
Dr. Scott Lee

Q&A Integration

As a clinical psychologist I'm required to receive a bunch of continuing education credits each year. At these presentations, I'm often amazed at the questions from the audience that follow truly terrific presentations. Colleagues must think of themselves quite insightful, enlightened and worthy of remaking the presentation for the rest of us!

While some "questions" appear more like treatises, others seem like "stump the presenter." Handling the Q&A session is like finishing the paperwork for the job; we may not look forward to it, but we're not finished until the job is completed. The Q&A session goes well when we remember this important point:

The Q&A is part of the presentation and, as such, has the same goals of the presentation: Connect with the audience, clarify your presentation message.

The Q&A time goes poorly when the audience is disconnected during inappropriate comments or when the presenter's message is lost in irrelevant ramblings. Most of the questions can be handled directly and briefly, maintaining a nice flow to the presentation. However, other questions present potential roadblocks that benefit from some care in the presenter's response.

While whole books have been written on this subject, I would just like to address a few possible Q&A roadblocks. Good luck on handling this part of the presentation!

A Closer Look...
- ### *The "co-presenter"*

   "I have things to say that everyone will want to hear."
   "Many are called, few are chosen" might be the motto of the "co-presenter." These audience members wish to take this opportunity to make their input the more significant presentation of the day. It's not so much that they didn't listen or appreciate what you had to say, it's more about your presentation as being an elegant segue into what they have been wanting to share for some time. Unfortunately, the rest of the audience generally does not appreciate someone who is usurping the stage at the moment, so your job is to get this person back in their seat and go on. While the temptation is to put them in their place

straightaway, the better techniques I have seen are direct but not belittling.

"You bring up some interesting ideas that perhaps we could talk about after the presentation this morning."

Or, "I am not sure what you mean. Could you restate your thought as a question?" They will not be able to ask a question because they have no question, but you gave them a chance and the audience appreciates that you did not beat up one of their own.

You, then, continue on with as much grace as possible. "Let's have the next question." You, and only you, are responsible for roping these wild cattle and returning them to the corral, **so keep it moving, answer in just a few sentences whenever possible, and be kind to those who may not be kind to you**.

▸ *Stump the presenter*

"I'm smarter than you are."

Perhaps you have seen verbal hooks dangled in front of a presenter as an audience member tries to draw the presenter into battle. One of the more frequent games I have seen is "Stump the presenter," where the only goal is to make the presenter look dumb. In this form of "one-upmanship," there is a direct attack on the pecking order, with the intent of elevating the audience member at the expense of the presenter. A question is asked which could only be answered by God, such as…

"So, according to your studies, when do you believe people begin to change their minds from previously held beliefs to accept the new understandings you are suggesting?"

Or, "What have been the greatest influences upon presentation techniques throughout the last century, and why have they been so influential?" Because these questions cannot be responded to briefly, if at all, and because they are not relevant to the presentation at hand, you, as the presenter, must unplug the audience member without insult.

Quick, polite responses are most effective, such as, "I don't have an answer for you, but perhaps you could find some more information on www.whatever.com," Or, "You ask a very interesting question, but because of time, we'll need to stay focused in this one area for today's session. Next question?" **You do not have to answer all the questions; you do not need to know everything there is to know about your subject. As a presenter, you do need to know something that might be helpful to the audience members. This is enough.** It's also ok if an audience member knows something you don't about your own material. Just don't get into a debate with the audience. Keep questions relevant and responses brief.

Remember, if you're in the business of providing helpful information to an audience, and the audience perceives you as gracious and vulnerable in allowing someone else to contribute succinctly, it's also a win for you.

◆ *Men are from Mars, women, boys, cats, dogs...*

The off topic question

Occasionally there is a well-intentioned audience question that is interesting but off-topic or threatens to take the Q and A down an unnecessary rat hole.

Skill #9 – Survive Q&A Sessions

> *You are discussing the need to relate to an audience in selling your ideas and an audience member questions you about the differences between men and women as highlighted in John Gray's book, Men are from Mars, Women are from Venus.*

While these sex differences are fascinating to most audiences, they are not relevant unless you the presenter make them so. The task with an off topic but interesting question is to build a bridge between the question and your presentation. In the example cited, you might respond, "I would imagine that an all female audience would respond differently than an all male audience to some presentations. Perhaps you might use more verbal material with a female audience or more audience group interactions. With males, you might use more images and individual audience interactions. This response pattern would be worthy of a little study. Large picture answers have more room for bridges, so stay general and leave out the details on these answers.

▸ "Excuse me, I wasn't listening. Would you kindly repeat your presentation?"
The back 12-steps question

A fourth type of problem question is one that asks you to restate your presentation as if the audience member was in a prolonged bathroom stop and didn't hear a thing you said. Your presentation is on "Using Adobe PhotoShop to Create Presentation Graphics" and during the Q&A session someone says,

"I didn't quite catch all of the presentation. Could you review how to use Adobe PhotoShop in making presentation templates?"

Before slinging your whiteboard eraser at the questioner or uttering course comments, take a deep breath and make one statement, your main point, so that everybody gets to hear it one more time. In other words, use the questions of the audience to further your aims of **connecting** (with the audience) and **clarifying** your presentation ideas.

"Good questions outrank easy answers."
– Paul A. Samuelson

Survival Summaries

- **Restate the question** so all can hear it clearly.

  Your answers make no sense if the entire audience didn't hear the question.

- **Limit your answers to under one minute**

  Stay on track. Don't go where the questions haven't taken you.

- **Know when to divert some questions to another time/place**

  As presenter, you control this process and need to change the venue for the answer if it threatens to dilute your core themes.

- **Use the questioner's name whenever possible**

    Personalizing a response to even a few of the audience members by using their name brings you closer to your audience.

- **Know exactly how much question and answer time you want to provide**

    Tell your audience up front, when and how much Q & A time will be provided.

- **Provide a follow-up opportunity for questions**

    Email addresses provide a good venue for future, less formal support.

- **Prepare a one-minute summary statement after Q & A**

    Leaving Q & A with out a clean close can make your presentation ending anti-climatic.

Survival Skill 10

"Character may be manifested in the great moments, but it is made in the small ones."
– Phillip Brooks

Understand Your Ultimate Strength

Over the last several decades, there have been several recognizable trains of thought created by this nation's greatest business thinkers. They seem to fall into several camps: those who simply define the trends and processes of the day, and those who take an inside/out look at how lasting change is fostered within an individual's hopes, goals and character.

These deep thinkers came full circle from the "fake it until you make it" fads of power ties and country clubs and tried to help us navigate the shifting sands of organizational growth in a new context. Ken Blanchard's *The One-Minute Manager* was one of the first pioneering works. Stephen Covey came along a while later and took a rare look at the essence of our personal development in *Seven Habits of Highly Effective People*. In the 90's, Peter Senge's *The Fifth Discipline* focused on how we tie into the collective power of individuals by understanding their goals supported by new relational tools. In all this, there are some common threads that speak to us as presenters.

Skill #10 – Understand Your Ultimate Strength

Rarely do you find presenters, both frequent and infrequent, who are successful through simply emulating someone else.

The idea that dressing for success, gesturing in the right way, standing in precisely the right place or using a particular electronic projector will pave your road to presentation success is a fallacy. **At its very core, presenting is not about body mechanics or lumens; rather it's about the process of creating relational touch points with an audience.** Your presentation is meaningful because your knowledge impacts them directly. Your experiences help your audiences understand their own better. Your personal stories create a clear context for the challenges they face. The graphics you use are the book illustrations that bring your storyline to life. This is not to say that your execution is not an issue. However, a preoccupation with form over substance is rarely memorable. Sexy graphics overlaid on top of a weak message is like putting lipstick on a pig. Good body mechanics without some personal context simply means the pig has learned to stand in a particular corner of the stall. The best technology in the world only means the pig now stands in a very bright spot light.

A few years back I took my daughter Amy to a Christmas concert featuring a nationally-recognized country gospel singer where 15,000 people were in attendance. Within the first ten minutes, the audience was endeared to this entertainer because of her casual interaction, southern drawl and vulnerability. She made you feel like she was sitting down and having a conversation with you in your living room. She had to deliver vocally (just like we need to deliver on our presentation promises) but the personal connection she created without the benefit of any direct eye contact was masterful.

I can hear what a few of you might be saying right about now. "I've never been a very good presenter" or "others present much better than I do." I want to challenge that. **I've seen audiences who are deeply engaged with a presenter who fell far short of an Anthony Robbins benchmark**. I've also experienced presenters whose neatly professional and inspirational message wore off a few hours later because there was little relational substance to accompany the fluff.

We all hold the keys to being not just average presenters but really good ones. Yes, for some it might take more work but the rewards are great both personally and professionally. So take this message to heart. Glean what you can from the ideas in the Survival Guide. Make continuous improvement a part of who you are in presenting and other areas of your life.

None of us are perfect presenters but contrary to contemporary thought, our lack of perfection is not a weakness at all; but for many presenters, their humaness becomes their ultimate strength.

Shrink Wrap
Dr. Scott Lee
Latitude of Acceptance

The 2000 presidential election represented a divided country: 50% vote for Al Gore, 50% vote for George W. Bush. Many in the nation were incensed that the vote of the Supreme Court, not the American people, ultimately picked the president. So when George W. got the nod, he had a difficult task. Do something immediately to connect with the country or face deepening the political split. His first actions were to choose political moderates for his cabinet with wide demographic representation. Of his first five choices, he nominated two blacks, a cuban, two women and a hispanic. Out of his entire cabinet, only two nominations represented the conservative right for which the republican party has been known. How come?

The answer lies in the psychological principle of "**latitude of acceptance**." There is a range of beliefs on every issue, and we as the American audience were not accepting of a message either far right or far left. Our "latitude of acceptance" for political leadership at this time was in the middle, perhaps from four to six on a scale of ten. Psychologists, and politicians, understand that unless you first identify with your audience, reaching into their latitude of acceptance, you will not be able to move them further to any other position. Therefore, President-elect Bush's first appointees were acceptable and began to solidify a divided country.

When each of us begins to present, we face a similar condition - the audience is separate from us and we need to connect. We must understand where the audience is at (in terms of what is acceptable) and first build a bridge to that place before moving further. Here is the key - all audiences are human, have wishes and dreams, hopes and feelings, pain and delight. **When you act as a human, merely sharing personal experiences, stories, etc., you connect with their latitude of acceptance.** As diverse as your audience might be, they will all meet at that important place. We each value our human experiences higher than our toys (well, most of the time), greater than our wealth, and more deeply than our corporate success. Our most significant substance to present is the stuff inside us, and if we are willing to be vulnerable building this bridge, then you will find your audience eagerly awaiting whatever else you have to say. Next time you present, acknowledge their "latitude of acceptance" and build a bridge from your greatest strength, your own human experience.

"Never give up, for that is just the place and time that the tide will turn."
– Harriet Beecher Stowe

Skill #10 – Understand Your Ultimate Strength

Online Survival Guide Resources

For more quick read resources on topics like jaggies, fonts, killer sales presentations, one way presentations turned into two way collaboration, picking good images and much more, check out a special Survival Skill supplement on the Distinction website at…

www.distinction-services.com/survive.html

Appendix

Presentation Terminology

Active matrix Computers and projectors have differing abilities to "refresh" the images produced. Active matrix technology refreshes the images so rapidly that a crisp, uniform image, free from "ghosting" is possible. This is especially noticeable in cursor movements and video images.

ANSI lumens This measure of light output of a projected image is a standard unit of measure & typically averages from corners & center.

Bitmapped graphics An image or graphic made up of individual pixels. Tend to be larger files and can originate from scanning photographs, screen captures or digital video. Also called a raster graphic.

CODEC A compression/decompression software component which translates video or audio between its uncompressed form and the compressed form in which it is stored.

Color depth We often hear references to 8 bit, 16 bit or 24 bit color. These measurements refer to how many unique colors are used to display the image. The more colors used, the smoother the color gradations will appear. Projector/computer combinations that can support 16-bit displays (65,500+color) will usually create smoother background gradients and more pleasing photographic or video images than 8-bit (256 color) technology.

Cross-platform The ability of applications or programs to run between PC & Macintosh platforms.

Appendix – Terminology

Digitizing The process of converting an image from analog format to digital data. For example, converting a videotape on a VCR to an MPEG file and storing it on a CD-ROM.

DPI Dots per inch was initially created to measure printer resolution, how many dots of ink the printer could lay down within an inch of paper space. However, today it is used as a more general & relative reference.

Font style This usually refers to characteristics added to a normal font, such as Bold, Italic, Underline, Shadow, Subscript, Superscript and Strikethrough. When embedding fonts – each style used requires a separate True Type file.

Frame rate The number of frames displayed per second during playback of an animation or digital video file.

GIF Graphics Interchange Format file extension. Used for graphics that can be defined using 256 colors or less. Often used for websites or web-based presentations.

Halogen bulbs These types of light bulbs produce a warmer image on screen. This bulb technology has been around for some time and is found in many different types of audio-visual projectors. When these bulbs burn out, they go immediately.

JPEG Joint Photographic Experts Group file extension. Can be saved with different levels of compression, so user can choose quality level (and file size). JPEG's work by looking at all existing data about an image, and then throwing out what isn't necessary or relevant to the actual image.

IR Remote Infrared remotes use invisible infrared light to send instructions to a computer. IR remotes have a shorter range than do RF remotes and must always be in "line of sight" with its receiver. Florescent lighting can impair performance.

Keystoning As an image is projected onto a screen or wall, the angle created can make your projected image appear to be narrower on the bottom than at the top. Most projectors today build in an automatic keystone correction to create a uniform image width top to bottom. Some projectors have the ability to manually adjust this characteristic while others provide more of a fixed correction solution.

LCD LCD displays utilize two sheets of polarizing material with a liquid crystal solution between them. An electric current passed through the liquid causes the crystals to align so that light cannot pass through them. Each crystal, therefore, is like a shutter, either allowing light to pass through or blocking the light

Lossless A term describing a data compression algorithm that retains all the information in the data, allowing it to be recovered perfectly.

Lossy A term describing a data compression algorithm that actually reduces the amount of information in the data, rather than just the number of bits used to represent that information. The lost information is usually removed because it is subjectively less important to the quality of the data or because it can be recovered reasonably by interpolation from the remaining data. MPEG and JPEG are examples of lossy compression techniques.

Metal halide bulbs These types of light bulbs produce a characteristically cooler image on screen. As these bulbs age, they tend to fade slowly over time. When the image on the wall doesn't seem to be as bright as it used to be and your projector brightness is already turned up, it's probably time for a new bulb.

Multimedia The combination of more than one media type to distribute and communicate information (text, audio, graphics, animation, and full-motion video).

Passive Matrix This older display technology is often recognizable by a subtle "ghosting" effect on screen during cursor movements. The images cannot refresh sufficiently fast to eliminate the effect. The good news is that although your older laptop may demonstrate this characteristic, the electronically

Appendix – Terminology

projected image can still be Active Matrix producing a clear-crisp image for your audience.

Pixel A pixel is the most fundamental element of a digital image. Pixels are arranged in rows and columns (each can be found on an x,y coordinate system) to define an image on a monitor, projector, or other output device.

Resolution The measure of detail in an image, usually expressed as the number of pixels in an image, or the number of dots per inch used by an output device. Higher resolution means smoother edges and more detail on things such as fonts and bitmapped images.

RF remote Radio frequency remotes use radio waves to transmit data between the remote and its base. RF remotes have a much greater range because radio waves can be transmitted through or around solid objects. It functions much like the antenna on your car radio.

RGB An acronym for red, green, and blue, which is a color model that uses the primary color values of a computer monitor to represent every color in the color spectrum. Every color has an RGB value.

Sampling The process of reading an analog signal at specific increments in time and storing the data as digital values.

Sans-serif font A type face that does not have serifs (tails). Sans-serif faces lend a clean, simple & highly readable appearance to presentations.

Scaling (the image) Simply refers to making the image larger or smaller while typically maintaining original aspect ratio.

Serif font Small decorative strokes that are added to the end of a letter's main strokes. Serifs improve readability by leading the eye along the line of type but can impair presentation legibility when used too small or in larger presentation venues.

"Stock" photography Typically digitized photographic images available on a CD or online who's usage is dictated by licensing agreements between buyer & seller. Stock photography can add a professional appearance to a presentation.

SVGA This 800x600 pixel dimension means there are 800 horizontal pixels and 600 vertical pixels that define the image on screen.

SXGA A 1280x1024 pixel dimension means there are 1280 horizontal pixels and 1024 vertical pixels that define the image on screen. This extremely high-resolution specification for computer and projector displays is most frequently required in intricate workstation-design setting, where maximum detail is essential.

Thumbnail A small version of an image that is used to quickly display an approximation of the contents of an image file.

TIFF Tag Interchange File Format. A very high quality file format associated with graphical images; also one of the largest in file size retaining a maximum amount of initial image information.

Vector-based art Graphic data composed primarily of representations of lines and outlines of objects, which can be compactly stored by specifying sets of key points. A computer application such as PowerPoint displays these graphics by interpolating the points between the key graphics. Vector-based art is nothing more than a mathematical equation, whereas bitmapped art is made up of individual pixels.

VGA 640x480 pixel dimensions means there are 640 horizontal pixels and 480 vertical pixels that define the image on screen. This older specification generally means that text will appear more "jaggy" and bitmap images like photos less uniform.

XGA 1024x768 pixel dimensions means there are 1024 horizontal pixels and 768 vertical pixels that define the image on screen. This very high resolution specification for computer and projector displays has eliminated jaggy text and made it possible to read even the smallest detail in spreadsheets and projected software screens.

Webcasting The use of the Internet to deliver content to typically decentralized audiences. These sessions can be hosted or non-hosted. Webcasting implies the use of more broad bandwidth media like animation and video with predominately a one way communication.

Web conferencing The use of the Internet to deliver content to typically decentralized audiences. Web conferencing suggests a potential two-way communication with an audience. Applications can include planning, product promotion and training.

PowerPoint Terminology

Action Buttons Preset buttons in PowerPoint allow the user to choose certain actions during their slide show. Examples of action buttons include Home, End of show, Forward, and Backward but can also facilitate a jump to an Internet location or application (.exe). There are many other preset buttons as well.

Color Scheme A set of eight colors called a "palette" that assigns colors to specific items within the presentation. Categories of color include Background color, Title text color, Text Color, Shadow Color, and four highlight colors for charts.

Custom Animation A dialogue box that allows the user to customize movement and introduction of on-screen elements.

Custom Shows A feature that allows users to customize which slides they want in a particular slide show. For instance, if you had 40 slides but in some instances only wanted to show 25 of them, you could specify a unique path through the presentation slides.

Distribute Creating an equal distance between two or more objects. PowerPoint has tools for distributing vertically or horizontally.

Grid Lines Dotted lines that appear when a user hits Ctrl-G inside PowerPoint. They help in measuring distances, as well as aligning various objects. For example, align-left several pictures by putting a vertical gridline where you want, and then move the pictures over until they "snap" to the grid.

Nudge Moving an item (picture, object, text box, or group) one pixel up, down, left, or right. It can be accomplished by selecting the item and pushing the arrow keys. The item will jump more than one pixel if the Snap Guides are on.

Placeholders Actual areas where designated items are to be put, such as a Title Placeholder or a Text placeholder. Placeholders refer to the box around the text & represent a default condition.

Quick Keys A set of helpful keyboard strokes to replace more time-consuming menu selections. (PowerPoint-Windows)

Control c	Copies a selected object to clipboard
Control v	Pastes objects in clipboard into work area
Control x	Cuts selected objects to clipboard
Control g	Turns on and off PowerPoint alignment grid lines
Control z	Undo
Control d	Duplicates selected object. Placement of duplicated object in relationship to their original sets the pattern that can quickly replicate a number of evenly spaced objects.
Control a	Selects all objects on screen
Control p	Prints
Control s	Saves the file

Appendix – Terminology

Slide Sorter View See presentation slides as if laid out on a light box. Slides can be rapidly moved, copied as well as effects assigned quickly. Also, slides from other presentations can be easily assembled.

Slide Master The slide that determines default conditions for every slide in the presentation. Examples of what can be standardized when viewing the slide master include background color or template, slide color scheme, layout of text placeholders, font style, color and size, and default animation of bullet slides. Also, background graphics or text placed in the Slide Master will be seen in the same place on all slides, but will not be editable while in Normal slide view mode.

Snap An invisible grid that items onscreen automatically "reach" for. Can be turned on or off within PowerPoint.

Title Master Similar to Slide Master, except this set of rules and layout apply to Title Slides when called out in Insert-New Slide & Title layout is selected.

"You can't wait for inspiration. You have to go after it with a club."
– Jack London

NOTES

"Would you persuade, speak of interest, not of reason."
— *Benjamin Franklin*

NOTES

"Talent is commonly developed at the expense of character."
– Ralph Waldo Emerson

NOTES

About the authors

Jim Endicott

Jim is a nationally recognized consultant, speaker and trainer specializing in professional presentation messaging, design, development and delivery. Jim's writing appears in **PRESENTATIONS** magazine, as well as many presentations-related websites. Jim also delivers seminars nationally on effective presentation design and delivery skills. His company, Distinction, provides consulting and presentation design services for major clients and leverages the Internet for delivery of design content and training.

Scott W. Lee, Ph.D.

Scott is a clinical psychologist who practices in Seattle, Washington. He specializes in interpersonal interactions and speaks and consults in the area of relational dynamics. As a psychologist, he shares a unique perspective on the psychology of influence and the issues of change with our audiences. When not seeing clients, speaking or writing, you'll find Scott on a mountain stream pursuing the elusive trout with his family or friends.

For information on seminar availability, authors can be contacted at Distinction Communication, 503-554-1203 or e-mail: **authors@distinction-services.com**